CALLED OUT OF DARKNESS

TESHAUNA L. ISAAC

BLACK OUT

CALLED OUT OF DARKNESS

TESHAUNA L. ISAAC

T&J PUBLISHERS

A SMALL INDEPENDENT PUBLISHER WITH A BIG VOICE

Printed in the United States of America by
T&J Publishers (Atlanta, GA.)
www.TandJPublishers.com

© Copyright 2022 by Teshauna L. Isaac

All rights reserved. This book or parts thereof may not be reproduced in any form, stored in a retrieval system, or transmitted in any form by any means-electronic, mechanical, photocopy, recording, or otherwise-without prior written permission of the author, except as provided by United States of America copyright law.

Bible Translations used: King James Version (KJV), New International Version (NIV), New Living Translation (NLT), English Standard Version (ESV), The Message Translation (MSG), Good News Translation (GNT), and The Amplified Bible (AMP)

Cover Design by Michael Corvin (https://corvin-bookcovers.com/)
Book Format/Layout by Timothy Flemming, Jr. (T&J Publishers)

ISBN: 979-8-218-03884-7

To contact author, go to:
www.teshaunaisaac.com
teshaunaisaac@gmail.com

Dedications

All Glory and Honor belong to God. I thank Him for calling me out of darkness into His marvelous light. Without His grace, the completion of this book would be impossible. Therefore, I give this book back to God that He may bless and multiply it, and it goes beyond where I have yet to travel and into the hands of those ready for an awakening!

I dedicate this book to those unsure of what life is all about and searching for the truth. You may think that you have done so much wrong that there is no way God would accept you with open arms into His Kingdom. But, I have Good News for you it's not too late!

To my Mother and Father, I dedicate this book to you for caring for me and helping me become the woman I am today. Thank you for your unconditional love and for always being there for me no matter what.

To my grandmother, who is sleeping in the Lord. I dedicate this book to you. She is the one who taught me how to pray and serve. She encouraged me never to give up and always hold on to God's unchanging hand.

To my sisters, I dedicate this book to you. I love you and want to thank you for supporting me in whatever I do. This book would not be if it were not for all of the things we experienced together.

To my children and grandbaby, I dedicate this book to you. You are one of the best gifts God has ever given to me. Unfortunately, moms don't always get it right but thank you for your patience and love. I love you, and the best is yet to come.

To my nephew Desmont, I dedicate this book to you. Auntie loves and misses you so much! I received strength from the Lord that I didn't know was possible until suddenly it was time for your return to the Lord.

To all my family and friends, I dedicate this book to you. Thank you for the love, support, encouragement, and prayers. I would not have been able to complete this assignment without you!

"But ye are a chosen generation, a royal priesthood, an holy nation, a peculiar people; that ye should shew forth the praises of him who hath called you out of darkness into his marvellous light."—1 Peter 2:9

Table of Contents

Introduction	11
Chapter 1: Unchecked Trauma	15
Chapter 2: A Dark Relationship	25
Chapter 3: A Prison Cell	37
Chapter 4: A Dark State Of Mind	53
Chapter 5: Inviting Evil	65
Chapter 6: Dethroning The Idol Of Self	79
Chapter 7: Walking In The Light	95
Final Words	113

Introduction

There are names for what I was dealing with that described my disruptive, impulsive behavior: Intermittent Explosive Disorder and Rage! Yes, there were times when problems arose in my life that I lacked self-control of my emotions and misbehaved. When extremely angry, I would fly into a fit of pure rage and possibly blackout. After I regained my focus, I noticed the damage I had caused. And that's the scary part. Getting into fights and not remembering everything that happened. Only by the recall of others would I know what I had done. My body would be on autopilot, fighting as if my life depended on it—throwing things, breaking things, hitting, biting, scratching, screaming or yelling. I was susceptible to using a baseball bat or brick to hit someone or something, grab a knife to stab, or worse.

One of my biggest fears was killing someone while in this state. Losing control of myself, I was liable to do anything. I heard the stories; I knew the risks. I can recall the case of a man who experienced the type of rage I did. He got so angry one day during an altercation with his wife he blacked out. When he awoke, he was horrified to find her lifeless body lying on the floor before him. It was discovered that he'd strangled the poor woman to death. Now that is a nightmare situation. I feared, one day, opening my eyes only to find some sharp, deadly object in my hand that I used to snuff out someone's life. And the thing that frightened me the most was knowing I was on the fast track to doing just that. I knew I had to make a change, and fast. I had to get a handle on myself before I did something stupid to someone else or even myself.

Oftentimes when angry, I would see red, my heart rate would be jacked (fight or flight), and murderous thoughts would run rampant in my mind. I was truly out of control. I would go crazy without any thought about the consequences. So, on the one hand, I felt justified in letting myself go, but on the other hand, I was always afraid that I would one day take things too far and find myself in serious trouble. And I eventually did—more on that later.

The reality is that the same darkness that overcame me when enraged was the same darkness that controlled my life. Even with my eyes open, I was blind and in the dark. I was in the dark when it came to my decisions and relationships. I also lacked an understanding of my identity and God's purpose, plan, and will for my life, and so much more. I was lost—that usually occurs when you walk around in the dark. When you walk in darkness, you end up in places you didn't intend to be. And the only thing you're left asking is, "How did I end up here?" When you lack a sense of direction for your life, that is the question you will ultimately ask.

INTRODUCTION

Unprocessed thoughts and feelings will cause you to harbor unhealed hurts and pains in your heart. When you ignore God's Spirit in your life by rejecting or rebelling against the process of being healed and delivered, your heart and mind don't function as God intended. Maybe your physical eyes never went black like mine, but your spiritual eyes are just as blind; this doesn't make it any easier. Spiritual blindness is just as, if not more, dangerous than physical blindness.

I would say I lived the majority of my life in the dark. My eyes were closed, my sight was blackened, my mind was in the wrong place, and my spirit was lost. Yes, I was lost. I had no sense of direction and had become a danger to myself and others. But thankfully, I discovered the source of what I was dealing with and addressed it. The results were phenomenal. I stopped reacting to situations and started taking control of them. I stopped having fits of rage that would cause me to blackout and learned to take control of my thoughts and actions. Furthermore, I gained a sense of direction and clarity in my life and discovered my true identity and purpose. But it all started the day I made a conscious decision to become the woman God wanted me to be.

In this book, I will show you how to come out of the dark just as I did. It doesn't matter what you're caught up in. And trust me when I tell you, there's a way out. You might not believe that, but it's true. If I came out of the darkness after many years of living in it, you can too. All you have to do is believe God wants you to be free and follow the steps I'm going to layout before you in this book.

It's your time! It's time for you to be free! There is a

BLACKOUT

light shining in the dark today; it is the light of truth and divine revelation, the light of God, and it's piercing the darkness at this very moment. So come with me, and let's step into the light so that you can see your bright future.

Chapter 1

UNCHECKED TRAUMA

"The Lord is near to the brokenhearted and saves
the crushed in spirit."—Psalm 34:18, ESV

MEDICAL EXPERTS AGREE THAT BLACKOUTS ARE usually caused by heavy trauma. The brain will go to great lengths to avoid pain, even shutting down. And that's what would happen to me. My brain would shut down when feeling overloaded with stress. And when I talk about stress, what I'm speaking of specifically is trauma.

According to the American Psychological Association (APA), trauma is "an emotional response to a terrible event like an accident, rape or natural disaster. ... Longer term reactions include unpredictable emotions, flashbacks, strained relationships and even physical symptoms like headaches or nausea." For me, the trauma I faced started in childhood. That's when I faced abuse of various kinds: psychological, emotional, physical, and sexual.

WHERE IT BEGAN FOR ME WHEN

I suffered the loss of my uncle at the age of four. He was murdered in the house I remember playing in. I was shown where his body lay; there was a bullet wound on the floor in that spot. As a little girl, I had no idea the impact that event would have on my life.

Another event that impacted my life was a series of sexual assaults that I experienced in elementary school, my third through fifth-grade years, by some of the boys in my classes. My dad had to go to the school several times and talk to the principal about what those boys were doing to me. They were constantly touching me without my permission. Although I didn't fully understand what they were doing to me, I knew it was wrong and still felt violated. Of course, they would get paddled by the principal, but not much else. However, the damage was already done to me psychologically and emotionally, and the effects thereof festered in my heart for years to come.

Experiences such as the ones I just mentioned caused significant damage to my self-esteem. I wrestled with feelings of unworthiness and a sense of powerlessness. The stories I began telling myself to explain these things were crippling. I blamed myself for the things done to me. I saw myself as a culprit and questioned myself. I perceived myself as weak and undeserving of love and respect. These beliefs became my subconscious programming.

It didn't help that my father wrestled with substance abuse, and his struggle would spill over into our home, causing constant arguments and fights between him and my mom

CHAPTER 1: UNCHECKED TRAUMA

and a slew of other problems, financially and otherwise. The disorder in my home caused me to live with the constant fear of my dad leaving us and never returning. I lived with the fear of abandonment all my life as a child; this kept me in a constant state of stress and paranoia, and it further aided in the stress I put on myself to "perform" for others' approval. As a child, I didn't think about the fact that my parents were having their own issues and failed to communicate properly and learn proper coping skills.

Alongside family trouble, bullying, sexual assaults, and the traumatizing murder of my uncle, my family and I experienced racial bigotry. There were several incidents, but one that stands out was when my mom, siblings, and I went shopping for Easter outfits. I can remember we stopped at Chick-fil-A to get some lunch. There was a sample of the food on display for tasting. My older sister walked over to get a piece; a White woman and her daughter were also about to get samples. When that woman saw my sister approaching, she told her daughter, "leave those for the monkeys!" But, of course, my mother was not having that. My mom went off on the woman, but a seed was planted in my mind at that moment.

I'd seen my mom deal with racial attacks. Once, I can remember her being accosted by several White men in a pickup truck. My mom had to pull out a baseball bat and threaten them to leave us alone. But, again, those were just a few examples of the racial bigotry we experienced.

Let me emphasize this point clearly: It's not what happens to you that matters the most; it's how you perceive what happens to you and what you tell yourself about what happens that matters the most. I developed soul wounds due to the lies I told myself and repeatedly rehearsed in my mind. My brain developed a defence mechanism to shield me from future events similar to the ones I'd experienced. Unfortunately, I had never processed these experiences properly; therefore, I lived life the wrong way.

I was a young lady looking for love—there was a hole in my soul that needed to be filled. And it's needful to mention that all of us need love. But I looked for love in the wrong places. I didn't know first, to seek God's love, and secondly, to love myself. I, instead, sought approval and validation from guys. Chasing these things landed me in precarious positions. For example, when I was thirteen and a half years old, I started dating a gang member. I felt accepted by that gang and started getting into trouble myself. I didn't realize the danger that I was putting my family and myself in; I just wanted love and acceptance.

By the time I was sixteen years old, I was pregnant. My son's father and I had broken up by the time my son was six months old. But desperate for love, I ended up getting married at nineteen-years-old. I became a mother of two before the age of twenty. However, I divorced that guy after only two years of marriage. I then remarried the same guy two years later, which turned out to be a huge mistake because, over the next four years of my life, I experienced constant infidelity and abuse. I put up with things I didn't have to and remained in situations I didn't need to be in because of the negative perception I had of myself and many unresolved issues concealed in my heart. I held onto a false sense of security, which those relationships

CHAPTER 1: UNCHECKED TRAUMA

provided—I'll talk more about this in a moment.

I'd developed a lifestyle of "react now" and "think later". I would get into fights and thus, end up with a criminal record. I actually feared going to prison. That was the last place I wanted to be. So I tried to keep myself busy in the gym to stay out of trouble. I'd also begun going to church. I would sit in the balcony and listen to the word preached, but I hadn't fully surrendered my life to Christ, to be honest. How can you surrender the things you're hiding and concealing? You can't. You have to first come out of denial about who you are and the things you're wrestling with, something I had yet to do; therefore, I failed to give God access to every part of me. I didn't surrender the regrets, disappointments, pain, trauma, and shame to Him. To me, those were things I could handle on my own. This thinking was my mistake.

Relying on my strength, I tried to change my life. I remember telling myself once I was not going out anymore because I felt like I would get into a fight, and there was nothing worth me jeopardizing my freedom. I felt like trouble followed me everywhere I went as if I attracted it. And to be honest, I did, but not in a spooky way. I attracted trouble because I trained myself to look for it. Know that you can train yourself to look for the negative or the positive things in others. It's up to you. I taught myself to look for the bad and negative. Certain keywords would stand out to me whenever people would speak to me, words I programmed my mind to pick up on. I trained my brain to listen for insults and sarcastic and rude comments. I stayed on the defense, ready for attack. I would ignore the ninety-nine comments to focus on the one rude comment, which made me feel justified in checking when necessary. There's an old saying, "Whatever you look for, you will find." I'd find trouble everywhere I went because I constantly looked for it. I had a radar designed to detect whenever a lady looked at me the wrong way. When that radar beeped, I jumped into action, ready to defend. I would allow little things to get to me, things I could have easily ignored. I didn't have to respond to every negative comment and address every mean stare. I didn't have to turn every mold hill into a mountain and blow things out of proportion. But I did this because I was hurt. Because I was hurt and still carrying offence in my heart from the past, I looked for reasons to justify being angry. I blamed others for my actions when I was the blame. It was my stinking attitude that kept me in a bunch of drama. And yet, the real problem wasn't the pain I carried and the negative coping mechanisms I relied on; it was the fact that I didn't seek the proper help for my problems; instead, I tried to suppress and handle things on my own. I pushed God and everyone else out and said, "I can handle this on my own." And that's what I did—I handle it. And in doing so, I ended up making a bigger mess of my life.

*

Little did I know that all of those negative experiences were transforming me over time. They were burrowing a hole into my heart and settling there like a rodent. Trauma has a way of getting trapped inside of your body like a toxic substance, and while there, it places great stress on your organs and body.

CHAPTER 1: UNCHECKED TRAUMA

This then leads to physical symptoms such as exhaustion, confusion, sadness, anxiety, agitation, numbness, dissociation (multiple personality disorder), confusion, persistent fatigue, sleep disorders, nightmares, fear of recurrence, anxiety focused on flashbacks, depression, and more. Trauma causes physical sicknesses in the body.

Medical science has discovered that over ninety percent of the sicknesses we experience are stress-related. Trauma keeps one's body in a permanent state of stress, which means they are on a one-way flight to the hospital.

Sadly, as children, no one teaches us about trauma. Very few people know what it is and how to deal with it. Most of what we know about trauma has emerged in recent years. So, for a long time, children and adults have suffered the effects of trauma without knowing it. Soldiers returning from the battlefields have suffered from Post Traumatic Stress Syndrome (PTSD) for years, many of them going unchecked and without help. Many of these individuals sought relief from the mental and emotional pain they were experiencing through drugs and alcohol.

Medical studies have revealed that trauma reshapes one's brain. Essentially, trauma leads to brain damage. Traumatized people aren't acting out intentionally in destructive ways; it is really that their brains have been reshaped and reprogrammed to engage in destructive patterns. That was my problem. I couldn't understand why I was so angry and always ready to fight.

It would take me many years before I discovered what I'm telling you now. I went on for far too long in the state

BLACKOUT

that I was in, and the result thereof was that I grew up an angry young lady, getting involved with things I didn't have any business getting involved with. I even began taking on a life of crime because I didn't know what my problem was—I didn't realize I had unchecked trauma in my life.

CHAPTER 1: UNCHECKED TRAUMA

MEDITATION VERSES

"'I will give you back your health and heal your wounds,' says the Lord. 'For you are called an outcast—'Jerusalem for whom no one cares.'" (Jeremiah 30:17, NLT)

"Behold, you delight in truth in the inward being, and you teach me wisdom in the secret heart." (Psalm 51:6, ESV)

"You keep track of all my sorrows. You have collected all my tears in your bottle. You have recorded each one in your book." (Psalm 56:8, NLT)

PRAYER

Dear Heavenly Father, I thank you for your love and grace. Today, I pray that you search my heart and bring to light every hidden thing in my life. You know the traumas I wrestle with and every secret thought that resides in my soul. Let your light shine upon them. I receive your light today, and I thank you for setting me free from the power of trauma in Jesus' name. Amen.

BLACKOUT

Chapter 2

A DARK RELATIONSHIP

> "Don't team up with those who are unbelievers. How can righteousness be a partner with wickedness? How can light live with darkness?"—2 Corinthians 6:14, NLT

I'm sure you've heard the phrase: "Looking for love in all of the wrong places". That just about summed up my life before coming to Christ. I was living in darkness; my mind was in a state of darkness, and my understanding was void. I felt empty within and didn't know why. I was looking for love but didn't know what love looked like, what it felt like, or where to find it. I'd seen nothing but dysfunction in my family growing up as a child. I witnessed domestic violence from a distance; it was happening to my family members. I'd experienced more of the mental and emotional abuse aside from the physical and sexual abuse I suffered at the hands of several of my peers. But it's that kind of environment I grew up in. I didn't know the truth of God's Word—what it teaches us regarding how to live and how to see ourselves. My perception of myself was wrong. And because I didn't understand who I was and what God's plan for me was, I ended up jumping into...

A BAD MARRIAGE

When you're living in darkness, you gravitate toward the wrong people. My soul was wounded from the rejection I experienced as a child, and therefore, I became bitter and hardhearted. As a result, I rejected that which was good for me and accepted that which was bad for me. If a guy wanted to get with me, I would size him up using the wrong measuring stick. He could have been a good man, but good men weren't fun and exciting enough for me. I was attracted to danger and abuse. I would look at a guy who wasn't the type I was looking for and say things about him like, "He's too quiet. He's too clingy. He looks like a punk. He's just not my type." I would find any reason to reject guys who weren't trouble to be around.

I'd seen dysfunction while growing up, so that's what I was attracted to—this was a subconscious longing. I mean, we all tell ourselves we want someone who will respect us, but is that really the case? If you've only witnessed abuse growing up, you might come to view abuse as an expression of love or become so familiar with it that you long for it. When it comes down to doing that which is right versus doing that which is comfortable to us, we usually lean in the direction of doing that which is comfortable, even if that which is comfortable is abuse, neglect, and mistreatment. People will rarely abandon their comfort-zones.

CHAPTER 2: A DARK RELATIONSHIP

For me, life was moving too fast. Again, my junior year in high school was different. I'd gone from running track, playing in the marching band, and cheerleading to being a teenage mom handling all of the responsibilities that came along with it—this was totally different from babysitting.

At the time, I was working at Wendy's part-time. My parents were crazy about my son; he was their first grandchild. They made sure my son and I didn't want for anything. As stated earlier, I broke up with the guy who was my son's father, but I still wanted someone to love, so I got into a relationship with a guy I believed was everything I needed and wanted. But I was nowhere near ready for a relationship.

Before long, I was announcing to others that I was getting married. I remember one of my cousins calling me and asking me to wait until I was finished with college first before getting married. She told me that if he loved me, he'd wait. But I didn't listen to her. I was thinking, *she has never been married, so what does she know*. Sadly, no one else tried to talk some sense into my head. I didn't think about the fact that this particular cousin was much older than I; she had just graduated from Clark University and did not have her first child until after completing her degree. She knew there was so much more about life that I had yet to experience, but I was too busy judging to take her advice.

What was I thinking? I was nineteen years old and wasn't wife-material. But I fell head-over-heels for a guy I'd met at the skating rink. Selfishly, I entered into a relationship with him, knowing he was already in a relationship with another woman. That should have been a serious red flag, a sign of things to come, but I wasn't concerned. I was simply concerned about myself and what I wanted. However, I later learned that if a guy will cheat *with* you, he'll also cheat *on* you.

A few weeks before our wedding, I ended up getting into a fight with his ex-girlfriend. I was steadily ignoring all of the signs this was the wrong relationship to be in. I was busy lying to myself the entire time about the situation, telling myself he would be faithful to me, we'd be too in love to let anything get between us, his ex-girlfriends were old news and more. I was simply desperate to be with someone. Furthermore, I was afraid that if I called the wedding off, I'd look bad in the eyes of those I told about the wedding. I was afraid they would judge me and talk about me for not being able to go through with it. I had propped up that relationship so that it became my identity; it validated me. Pretending that I'd found love, true love as if I'd experienced some huge accomplishment. And now, not getting married would be the ultimate embarrassment for me.

In the end, I'd sacrificed so much just for a facade. I'd always dreamed of a big, beautiful wedding in a sanctuary complete with bridesmaids, decorations, smiling family and friends, and all of the other small things that make such a moment memorable. However, I settled for a small, shotgun wedding in a small wedding chapel in Las Vegas. Everything felt so rushed and so off. But I sucked it up and continued to lie to myself about everything.

During the first two years of being with him, we experienced a rocky relationship. We argued and verbally attacked

CHAPTER 2: A DARK RELATIONSHIP

each other; it was a toxic environment, an abusive one. Alongside this was my husband's constant cheating. He was now doing to me what he had done to his ex. When I first met him, he claimed he was separated from his ex and was waiting for her to move out of his house. He claimed that he was living in the basement of his house until she moved out. When we got together, he started cheating with other women, and the lie he would tell them was that he was in the middle of getting a divorce and that he was living in the basement. In reality, he'd be in the basement so he could talk on the phone with his mistresses.

My marriage eventually came to an end. But even then, I didn't know how to walk away and move on. I stayed longer than I needed to begin with, remaining put even when the trust, attraction, and fun were gone. In the end, my marriage reminded me of the movie *The War of the Roses*.

I was concerned about what everyone thought of me. Furthermore, I wondered how I would make it as a single mother of three. My self-esteem was even more shot after being told nobody would want me by my ex. While in the relationship, I didn't have to pay any bills, so all I did was shop. I'd never taken the time to establish myself and learn how to stand on my own two feet. I went straight from living with my parents to living with my husband.

My mom saw the chaos that was taking place in my house; she knew what my husband was doing to me. She tried earnestly to persuade me to move back in with her and my dad, but I did not. I was tired of moving. I had moved so much during our marriage, separating for weeks, even months at a time from my husband, that I just left most of my clothes packed in garbage bags. I had them ready to move at any time, but I was tired of constantly moving. Also, my husband would come and make empty promises, claiming that if I returned home with him, things would be different. I'd take his word for it, only to get disappointed again...and again. He'd simply return to his lying, cheating, and abusive ways every time I returned home.

I remember trying to work through my first marriage. My husband would claim he was no longer cheating, and I so desperately wanted to believe him, but something inside of me told me not to. He would leave too many clues confirming he was lying. In one case, I did some detective work checking his tracks to see if he was being truthful. That day, he was supposed to be working. Instead, I discovered he was over at another woman's house when he should've been working. He was sloppy with it, too, parking his vehicle right in front of her house, and he had personalized plates, so there was no way he could deny it was him! That all took place during my day off at work. I rode up the street and turned down an alley so I wouldn't be seen riding past his mistress house. That's when my car got stuck in some snow. I certainly didn't want to call for help since I was stuck in an alley across the street from my husband's mistress's house—I didn't want to draw any attention to myself. So I did everything I could to try and get unstuck. I ended up causing an electrical fire in the car. One of her neighbors saw the dilemma I was in and was nice enough to help me out. I then drove the car home as fast as possible. I felt so foolish at the time. I was stalking a man I knew was

CHAPTER 2: A DARK RELATIONSHIP

lying and, while doing so, damaged my car, jeopardizing my life in the process. And yet, after all of that, I still stayed with that man.

I had a mountain of evidence of his affairs but wouldn't leave. I never thought I would find myself rambling through a man's clothes and car and checking the numbers in his beeper and voice mail just to see if he was cheating on me. I constantly felt embarrassed and like I'd lost my dignity. I began to do devious things to get back at him. For example, I would give him the silent treatment and then leave the house without communicating to him where I was going. I would leave and go to the library; at the time, I was working part-time and going to school full-time; this was driving my husband mad. You see, cheaters usually accuse others of doing what they do, so my husband started to suspect I was cheating on him. But I wasn't cheating; I just wanted him to think I was cheating.

One day, I left the house in a hurry without saying a word to him. As soon as I left, he left. This particular day, I had the day off of work. I remember my ex leaving out of the house angry because I wasn't communicating with him about my whereabouts. He pulled out of the driveway, drove down the street and was idle at the stop sign. Suddenly, he put the car in reverse and drove backwards down the road. At that moment, I was pulling out of the driveway to go my way. That's when I noticed his car coming my way, and he wasn't slowing down either. He ended up hitting my truck with his car. He was angry when he got out of the car, but he chose to do what he did. However, I knew what I was doing: I attempted to drive him mad with suspicion. I wanted him to feel what I was feeling. And I knew exactly how to press his buttons.

I began blaming myself for his cheating because I wasn't doing my duties as a wife. I would gather evidence of his affairs by snooping through his things and then confront him with it, thinking that if he knew he was busted, he would quit, but that didn't work. I had the fantasy that he'd return to being the man who said yes to me while standing at the altar, but who was I fooling. Furthermore, he was that man—when I met him, he was cheating with me on another woman. But when living in darkness, you can't see; you're blind. You make foolish decisions because you don't have God's Holy Spirit. So you go from one wrong decision to another, stringing yourself along the way with a bunch of lies you tell yourself.

After our second divorce, I felt nervous and afraid, not knowing what to do with myself and our kids. I had to figure out what to do to take care of them. I had to figure out what to do with myself; this was something new to me.

There is something about breaking up. You never expect it to happen, and it knocks the wind out of you when it does. I was now the ex expecting to have the same benefits I had when we were married. Again, I was now responsible for paying all the bills, handling the maintenance, grocery shopping and cooking, and everything else. I no longer had someone to share these responsibilities with. But the worse part for me was dealing with the new girlfriend.

It didn't take long for my ex to hook up with a new girlfriend. My ex and I shared joint custody of our kids, and

CHAPTER 2: A DARK RELATIONSHIP

that was hard to deal with because my kids had to go over to his place and be around his new girlfriend, who was allowed to mistreat them. I felt like my children had to suffer because of me when they were at their dad's house.

It would have been incredibly selfish of me to ignore the plight of my kids, to turn away from their suffering and the mistreatment they endured. But I had to learn how to handle the situation the right way—I had to learn how to place the problems in God's hands through prayer. I had to learn how to get myself out of the way. Before, I would disrespect my ex and his new girlfriend by giving them a piece of my mind—acting out of anger would only worsen the situation and prevent God from working things out on my behalf. However, when I stepped aside and let God heal my heart, I began to forgive my ex and pray for him instead of trash-talking and harboring thoughts of revenge. When I stopped blaming him for everything and calling him crazy, among other things, and focused on releasing my pain to God and trusting He would work things out, that's when a weight lifted off my shoulders. I began to see God work things out for my children and I.

I began to wisen up the more I turned to God. For example, it started to dawn on me just how selfish I'd been when acting foolishly. Before, at times, I would go to my ex's house to drop my kids off, and while there, I'd get out of the car and confront my ex, and that's when all hell would break loose. The two of us would often get into heated arguments; we fought a few times. Sometimes, I would take my friends with me when doing this—their presence was to ensure that my ex wouldn't do anything too drastic or crazy. Reflecting, I realized how much I had placed my friend in harm's way. She had to get between me and my ex during some of the fights. One time she was nursing an injury of her own and did not need to be involved in our mess. I could have endangered her with my reckless behavior.

    I began to ask myself, *why didn't I stay in the car? Is it that I want attention? Is it that I want to prove a point? Do I want to control my ex and be in total control of the situation?* My true motives were coming to the surface. I began to examine myself, realizing that none of what I was doing was justifiable in the eyes of God. I allowed my hurt to dictate my actions in the situation rather than listening to the Holy Spirit's voice. And now, I was beginning to take ownership over my actions, and I began to focus on finding solutions rather than playing the blame game.

*

It would take plenty of time, self-reflection, brutal honesty with myself, and forgiveness for my heart to heal and break the cycle of bad relationships. I needed to take the spotlight off of others—my ex, his girlfriend, and more—and cast that light on my soul, letting God highlight my issues, motives, traumas, and internal beliefs about myself. Rather than wasting my time praying for God to change my ex, I finally started asking God to change me.

CHAPTER 2: A DARK RELATIONSHIP

MEDITATION VERSES

"'Be ye not unequally yoked together with unbelievers: for what fellowship hath righteousness with unrighteousness? and what communion hath light with darkness? And what concord hath Christ with Belial? or what part hath he that believeth with an infidel? And what agreement hath the temple of God with idols? for ye are the temple of the living God; as God hath said, I will dwell in them, and walk in them; and I will be their God, and they shall be my people. Wherefore come out from among them, and be ye separate, saith the Lord, and touch not the unclean thing; and I will receive you, And will be a Father unto you, and ye shall be my sons and daughters, saith the Lord Almighty." (2 Corinthians 6:14-18)

"Never pay back evil with more evil. Do things in such a way that everyone can see you are honorable. Do all that you can to live in peace with everyone. Dear friends, never take revenge. Leave that to the righteous anger of God. For the Scriptures say, 'I will take revenge; I will pay them back,' says the LORD. Instead, if your enemies are hungry, feed them. If they are thirsty, give them something to drink. In doing this, you will heap burning coals of shame on their heads. Don't let evil conquer you, but conquer evil by doing good." (Romans 12:17-21, NLT)

Prayer

Dear Heavenly Father, I thank you for your love and protection over my life. You are able to see danger far ahead of me, therefore, I trust you in every situation. Continue to lead and guide me to the right people, the ones you have predestined to be in my life. Also, work on my heart. Heal me from any wounds I've sustained through bad relationships. I release every pain to you and curse the root of bitterness in my life. I choose instead to love others. Teach me how to love others as you do. I forgive those who have hurt me and release them into your hands so that you can heal them and set them free from any bondage and entanglement that is preventing them from walking in your perfect will for their lives. I thank you and pray this in Jesus' name, Amen.

Chapter 3
A PRISON CELL

"Bring me out of prison, that I may give thanks to your name! The righteous will surround me, for you will deal bountifully with me."—Psalm 142:7, ESV

As I explained in the previous chapter, I dealt with unchecked, unrecognized trauma in my life—everything from sexual assaults to the fear of abandonment and more. But unfortunately, I didn't know how to deal with these incidents in my life and process them in my mind, and consequently, I became controlled by that trauma. As a result, I ended up in harmful situations. And that's what an unhealed heart will do to you: put you in the wrong places. Then, with your trauma and negative thinking, you will invite and settle for negative things in your life. That's what happened to me.

For years, I harbored negative thoughts about myself. I believed I was destined to live a life of crime at one point. Then, again, I started dating a gang member as a teenager. I was already living in a rough community divided into gang territories. There was the Crip gang in my neighbourhood, and several blocks over were the Bloodz.

Being involved with a gang meant that I was bringing death to my family's doorstep. At first, the gang life seemed fun to me. It was fun hanging out with different guys and girls who did whatever they wanted and didn't care about the consequences; it is so ironic that if my parents knew what I was doing, they would have grounded me. Furthermore, I craved the sense of security the gang brought me. I didn't realize it then, but I was basing my decisions on fear and insecurity, and the gang life was incapable of providing me with what I desired. I would soon discover that the gang life provided only a false sense of security as friends were being killed or sentenced to prison; that's when my eyes opened, and I realized this wasn't a game.

I defied my mom's instructions of not going to cars to talk to guys in one incident. Instead of my boyfriend coming into the house, I went to the car to speak to him. While standing by the car, another guy ran up on a hill just steps away from the vehicle and began shooting at my boyfriend. Just like that, I could have died —I was practically in the guy's line of fire. I screamed and ran, but it was only the grace of God that kept me.

One night, I put my entire family in danger. First, my family was awakened because our dog would not stop barking. When I looked outside, I noticed a U-Haul parked on the side of our house. Inside were several guys with loaded guns. My newborn son and I were marked for death because my

CHAPTER 3: A PRISON CELL

son's father was associated with a guy whose girlfriend was missing—the girl's family wanted to retaliate. They figured my son's father was responsible for her death, and therefore, they would take his girlfriend and child away from him (my son and I). The only reason my house didn't get shot up that night and everyone inside killed was one of the guys carrying out the hit was my cousin, and he recognized our house.

Being associated with dangerous people kept me in danger. I was constantly watching my back, looking over my shoulder, fearing someone would run up on me and deliver me a bullet with my name on it. Unfortunately, that's what living in darkness will get you.

But there are other places where living in darkness landed me. Unfortunately, one of those places was the prison.

THE FIRST ARREST

One of the most embarrassing moments of my life was the day I was arrested while at my job. I was working as a bank teller. To be handcuffed in front of my coworkers, the customers, and my employer was humiliating. I felt like I would die and wished I was invisible. Sitting in the back of the police car while everyone's gaze fell upon me was equally as painful. I never wanted to show my face over there again after that.

Why was I being arrested? I'll honestly admit it was due to my lack of tolerance for mess! I had no problem making it clear that I would not be disrespected. I enjoyed making my point clear to folks who thought they were getting over me. Arguments that escalated to fights were justified; I would tell myself it was the other person's fault. I always had an excuse for doing and saying things I shouldn't have done or said, but that day, my antics finally caught up with me.

My husband at the time was having an affair with a particular young lady, and when I found out about it, I decided to handle it the wrong way. Instead of turning to God in prayer and asking Him for His wisdom in the matter, I decided to confront the lady. I chose to take matters into my own hands. I was ignorant, wanting to control other people's actions and force an unfaithful man to stop cheating on me. Furthermore, I couldn't control other women and prevent them from wanting my husband. I should have turned to God and allowed Him to speak to and convict my husband's heart; better yet, I should have left that relationship, realizing I was dealing with a guy who wasn't ready to be committed. As the Bible says, "Can an Ethiopian change the color of his skin? Can a leopard take away its spots? Neither can you start doing good, for you have always done evil" (Jeremiah 13:23, NLT). With that being said, you can't change a cheater. You can't make a player become an honest person. You have to keep your eyes open and be aware of what you involve yourself in. Realize that your actions and choices are your own, including jumping into a relationship that is bad for you.

The Bible says, "So don't bother correcting mockers; they will only hate you. But correct the wise, and they will love you" (Proverbs 9:8, NLT). This goes along with the saying: *If you want to make an enemy, try to correct a fool.* It would take me years to learn this. I'd played the fool when my cousin tried to talk me out of getting married in the first place: rather than listening to her sound advice and thinking about her

CHAPTER 3: A PRISON CELL

argument, my eyes remained closed, refusing to see the truth she was sharing with me. I wasn't ready to get married, but I didn't want to hear it. Similarly, I should have realized I was married to a person content with playing the fool. He didn't want to change and do the right thing. He didn't want correction. And when I confronted the lady he was having an affair with, she didn't want to listen and understand. It wasn't my place to force people who didn't want to do right to do right. My responsibility was to move on and count it as a loss—or better yet, count it as a gain since I was gaining freedom from a toxic relationship.

But that's not what I did. I stayed there and escalated the situation by making a phone call to punish the lady and end the affair. I thought I could flow with my emotions and do whatever I wanted, but I later found out it didn't work that way. That lady told the police I threatened her life, which I didn't. She told them she feared for her safety but left out the fact she was messing with a married man and was afraid to deal with the wrath from the wife. My zero-tolerance policy for mess was enforced, and now, I was in handcuffs for it.

After that incident, you'd think I learned my lesson and began practicing more self-control, but I didn't. I continued to play the fool. I continued to let my emotions dictate to me in every situation rather than dictating to my feelings what I was going to do. I continued to let my anger get the best of me and cause me to say and do things that got me in hot water. As my dad would say, "A hard head makes a soft butt." I had a hard head and was aligning myself to pay a high price for my actions.

HARVEST TIME

I'd gotten away with a lot in my life, and this is perhaps one of the reasons I ended up in a place no one in their right mind would make reservations to stay. I believed I would always get off the hook when doing wrong. My dad would tell me, "You are not getting away with anything," but I didn't understand him then. I'd done many crazy things while a teenager, from gang activities and more. I'd spent plenty of time fighting, threatening others with violence, and even committing minor offenses such as breaking traffic laws: speeding, running red lights, and more. But, for the most part, I never got caught or did any hard time in jail. I thought I was getting away with my reckless ways. However, I didn't realize that I was setting a trap for myself. Every time I tried to manipulate the law, I was digging a grave for myself. I was simply deceiving myself. I'd forgotten that there was one individual watching everything I did and kept a thorough record of all my wrongdoings: God. A warrant for my arrest was issued from Heaven.

There were times when I wondered if God was watching what I was doing. Looking back, I can see that Satan was leading me down the road of darkness toward destruction. He was deceiving me by planting thoughts in my mind that caused me to feel comfortable with my sins and wrongdoings. In one incident, I wondered if God was looking down upon me. I can remember distinctly hearing a voice say clearly, "He's not paying attention to you." That was the enemy's voice, but I didn't know it then. The enemy had me thinking there were no consequences for my actions. This is how he deceives the multitudes and even destroys entire nations and

CHAPTER 3: A PRISON CELL

civilizations: he tricks people into thinking there are no divine consequences for sin. *Live however you want to live*, he says. *Do whatever you want to do—there's no Hell, only Heaven. Forget the Bible and God's standards; create your way and live life on your terms. Smoke, drink, have sex with whoever you want, lie, steal, or even kill. It's all good. You're not doing anything wrong.* That's what the enemy says to us, but that's a lie. The Bible tells us that "the wages of sin is death," which means eternal separation from God (Romans 6:23). This separation refers to eternal damnation, otherwise known as Hell (Revelation 21:8; Matthew 10:28).

The Apostle Paul explained,

> "Live a life filled with love, following the example of Christ. He loved us and offered himself as a sacrifice for us, a pleasing aroma to God. Let there be no sexual immorality, impurity, or greed among you. Such sins have no place among God's people. Obscene stories, foolish talk, and coarse jokes—these are not for you. Instead, let there be thankfulness to God. You can be sure that no immoral, impure, or greedy person will inherit the Kingdom of Christ and of God. For a greedy person is an idolater, worshiping the things of this world. Don't be fooled by those who try to excuse these sins, for the anger of God will fall on all who disobey him. Don't participate in the things these people do. For once you were full of darkness, but now you have light from the Lord. So live as people of light!" (Ephesians 5:2-8, NLT)

Whenever people tell you there are no consequences for continually living an ungodly lifestyle, don't listen to them—they're lying. There are consequences. And the eyes of the law may not see you, but God sees you, and He will judge you if you don't repent. So you're never getting away with wrongdoing. Never!

The sad thing about listening to Satan is that he will always instruct you on how to get into a mess, but he'll never instruct you on how to get out of it. He'll encourage you to break rules that were designed to keep us safe and make life livable for us all. He will make you believe that rules are restricting and oppressive. For me, he primed me to resent authority. I didn't like being under anyone's authority. I would buck and rebel whenever an authority figure tried to correct and instruct me. I simply hated the idea of being told what to do. I believed I was above the rules, and they didn't apply to me. I thought I was untouchable and invincible. Again, that was a satanic deception that cost me.

I'd never talked to anyone about my fear of being incarcerated. That fear was deeply engrained in my conscious mind. Maybe it was due to too many stories or movies I'd seen; whatever the case, being sentenced to prison was one of my biggest fears. I knew myself—my temper and habits—and I constantly felt that I might one day go overboard and "catch a case" that would send me away for a long time, so as time progressed, I tried to change myself, which didn't work. Again, I tried to channel my energy and aggression in the gym, but that didn't stop me from getting into trouble. Whatever I tried

CHAPTER 3: A PRISON CELL

didn't work. I realized the habits I'd developed throughout my life were now directing my life to a place I didn't want to go. Sure, I could have developed different habits while young because I kept doing the wrong thing and getting away with it. I didn't see the damage I was doing to myself or the future I was creating for myself. I didn't realize I was reinforcing bad habits, and bad habits were carefully crafting the very future I feared the most.

An old saying: You create your habits, and your habits will turn around and create you. That's true. Eventually, when you practice doing good, "good" will become a normal way of life for you. You'll find yourself handling conflicts, treating people, and even perceiving yourself and the situation the right way. I saw meekness as a weakness for so long and believed it was better to be feared than respected. So I carried this "you'd better not cross me and tick me off" attitude, just waiting for wrong advances toward me. I walked around with a chip on my shoulder, thinking that being a defensive person was the way to survive. The whole time I was doing this, I planted seeds of destruction in my life.

The Bible says, "Guard your heart above all else, for it determines the course of your life" (Proverbs 4:23, NLT). The condition of your heart determines the state of your life. Your future, the places you find yourself in, isn't determined by the people around you. It isn't the "White man" who's holding you back, the "system" that's keeping you poor, your family that's why you're living a defeated life; the reason you are where you are is because of the seeds you sow into your heart. It's what you constantly tell yourself. Your words are what settle in your heart. Words are seeds. That's why the Bible says, "The tongue has the power of life and death, and those who love it will eat its fruit" (Proverbs 18:21, NIV). If you're wise, you'll start sowing good seeds today. You'll begin doing what David suggested in Psalm 119:11 and begin storing the Word of God in your heart so that you won't live your life in error and make foolish decisions. Remember, what you place in your heart forms the habits and beliefs that control your life. So if you spend your days talking mess about others, watching mess on television, or listening to mess on the radio and social media platforms, don't be surprised when your life ends up being a mess. All I can say is you reap what you sow. Whatever you sow into your heart is reflected in your life. Your life reflects what's in your heart.

Galatians 6:7 says, "Don't be misled—you cannot mock the justice of God. You will always harvest what you plant" (NLT). God is loving, but He is also just. If you sow evil, that's what you'll reap. If you keep planting evil thoughts in your heart through entertainment, that's what will manifest in your life. If you keep looking at things like porn and violence on screen, that's what will come out of you when the time comes. Eventually, if you mistreat people, you'll reap what you've sown and find yourself being mistreated. This is called divine justice, and you can't escape it.

No, I couldn't pick the circumstances I encountered and the things that were done to me, but I could determine my response to these things and choose to walk down a different path. I could have sown other words and thoughts into my heart and shaped a different set of beliefs. You can't control life, but you can control your attitude. My decision was to shape the wrong attitude. That was my choice.

Now, here's a very interesting revelation from God's Word: Proverbs 10:24 says, "What the wicked dread will overtake them; what the righteous desire will be granted" (NIV). Did you read that? When you're wicked (meaning you're deliberately walking in rebellion towards God in your life), the thing you fear the most will become your reality. It's like the devil is giving you glimpses of where he's taking you. Remember, fear is produced by the imagination—it's what you picture happening to you that strikes fear in your heart. You keep seeing yourself getting shot, dying in a car accident, getting mugged and killed, dying from an overdose, being arrested and sent away for life, losing your family, losing your health, dying from sickness and disease, losing your mind, losing great opportunities, embarrassing yourself and becoming a public disgrace, and more. These are all images that keep playing in your mind. These will become your reality when you choose to align yourself with Satan rather than submit to God, follow His plan, and walk in His righteousness. However, when you submit to God and seek His face, choosing to live according to His Word, the Bible says the desires you have in your heart will be "granted" to you by God. He will answer your prayers and bless you with that business you've always wanted, the success you desired, the house, the car, the financial stability, the wonderful spouse and kids, and the blessed life. God will honor you because you honor Him. It's that simple. It's not complicated. Satan desires to bring death and destruction upon you, as was stated by Jesus in John 10:10, which says,

"The thief's [Satan] purpose is to steal and kill and destroy" (NLT). However, Jesus said in that same verse that God desires to give you "a rich and satisfying life." When you align yourself with God, He will provide you with visions of yourself walking in incredible blessings, experiencing healing and breakthroughs, receiving elevations you don't qualify for, and promotions you don't deserve. God will produce an expectation of good things to come inside of your anticipation—this is hope. He will cause you to have visions of a bright future, whereas Satan will cause you to have visions of a bleak future.

Who are you going to submit to?

PRISON BLUES

One day, I went too far. I got into a fight with a woman, and I went overboard. I remember the judge's words to me in court: "You haven't been in trouble in six years, but one hit could have killed this woman." And he was right—I could have killed that woman. I wasn't thinking about the damage I would have caused to her and her entire family—the people who love her. And for what? Because she looked at me a certain way? Because she said something I didn't like? Is that any reason to end a life, rob a child of a mother, a parent of a daughter, or a husband of a wife? That was it. The judge had enough. He was sentencing me to prison this time.

This might sound strange to some people, but I thank God for my prison experience. I had an opportunity to examine my life, character, and behavior while incarcerated. I was in this dark place with others who were worse than me, who truly lacked a conscience and wouldn't hesitate to kill.

CHAPTER 3: A PRISON CELL

I couldn't just go off and act a fool in there; I had to practice more self-control. I was separated from everything I'd ever known.

My family wasn't there to help me. My lawyer couldn't get me off the hook this time. My friends couldn't do anything for me. But, this time, God had me right where He wanted me. I had no one else to turn to besides Him. And that's what I began to do.

I can recall a vision God gave me a few months before my sentencing. I saw myself in a beautiful green pasture, and I saw the hand of God upon me while there, letting me know I was in His hand. When I saw that vision, it didn't make sense to me. But, once I was sentenced, I found out what that vision meant. Although, while in prison, there were some crazies around, had I handled things there the way I did on the streets, I'd never gotten out of there, or I would have ended up dead. It was too easy to fall into the trap of temptation. But God was able to teach me His ways while there.

While waiting in the Lucas County jail, I listened to others talk about prison life; one story stood out. Once you arrive at the prison, I heard you could get hit as soon as you get off the bus! I was still new to this surrendering my life to Jesus thing, and I wasn't sure I would be able to resist hitting someone back if they hit me. So I began to pray and ask God to protect me, I was honest and told God I knew the right thing to do, but I didn't think I was there yet. A scripture came to mind while on my way to Ohio Reformatory for Women (ORW); it said, "But I tell you, do not resist an evil person. If anyone slaps you on the right cheek, turn to them the other cheek also" (Matthew 5:39, NIV). Now, that's not saying you can't defend yourself and your family, but what Jesus was saying was we should always seek peace in every situation. Peace, not chaos, should be our goal in every conflict. We should ask God for His wisdom to resolve issues the right way, knowing that our anger "does not produce the righteousness God desires" (James 1:20, NLT). So when we allow our anger to take control, we'll always produce the wrong results. Therefore, before you act or say anything out of anger, take a moment to sit back, relax, and then pray and place the situation in God's hands while asking Him for wisdom to produce the right results. He'll answer you if you call upon Him. He wants to give you wisdom. He said to ask Him for it, and He'll give it to you freely (James 1:5).

Yes, I was tempted in prison to get into fights, but the Holy Spirit was there the entire time, speaking to me and helping me to avoid situations I didn't need to be in. So many days, I cried out to God to release me from that place, but in the same breath, I asked Him not to allow me to leave prison the same person I was before getting locked up. I didn't want to be the old me.

Before prison, my prayers were centered around me: I would tell God what I didn't like, what I was going to do, and what I wasn't going to do. But one day, while in the shower, I had a spirit of humility come over me, and I began to lift my hands to God and say, "God, I will do whatever you want me to do, say whatever you want me to say, and go wherever you want me to go!" I began to let God take control. And after doing so, I began to experience His presence even more. I can

CHAPTER 3: A PRISON CELL

recall one incident. I was about to get into a fight with another lady when I distinctly heard the voice of the Holy Spirit tell me to "Shut up!" That startled me. I heard His voice clearly; it was a sharp rebuke. And I did—I shut up rather than running my mouth more and causing the situation to escalate. And by following that simple instruction, I deescalated the situation and spared myself a great deal of pain. I realized my ego and the Holy Spirit couldn't sit on the throne of my heart at the same time. Sure, by withholding my tongue, I felt weak, like I punked out; I felt embarrassed for a moment, but then I began to feel a sense of joy because I practiced self-control for the first time and reacted to the situation differently. I could sense now that I was becoming a different woman, a new person, and my way of thinking was changing. I was excited to be walking in an answered prayer. I was changing, little by little, slowly but surely. And I could tell this was God's way of saving me from an early grave. Finally, in one of the darkest places on earth, I began to see the light.

Meditation Verses

"'See to it that no one takes you captive by philosophy and empty deceit, according to human tradition, according to the elemental spirits of the world, and not according to Christ." (Colossians 2:8, ESV)

"For bodily exercise profiteth little: but godliness is profitable unto all things, having promise of the life that now is, and of that which is to come." (1 Timothy 4:8)

"If someone has a hot temper, let him take the consequences. If you get him out of trouble once, you will have to do it again." (Proverbs 19:19, GNT)

"Wherefore the law was our schoolmaster to bring us unto Christ, that we might be justified by faith. But after that faith is come, we are no longer under a schoolmaster. For ye are all the children of God by faith in Christ Jesus." (Gal 3:24-26)

Prayer

Dear Heavenly Father, I thank you for your truth and revelation. I thank you for correcting me when I'm wrong. You chastise those whom you love. I receive your correction today in my life. Continue to develop me into the person you created me to be. Mature me so that my actions are pleasing in your sight, in Jesus' name. Amen.

Chapter 4

A DARK STATE OF MIND

> "We use God's mighty weapons, not worldly weapons, to knock down the strongholds of human reasoning and to destroy false arguments. We destroy every proud obstacle that keeps people from knowing God. We capture their rebellious thoughts and teach them to obey Christ."
> —2 Corinthians 10:4-5, NLT

The term "nervous breakdown" is often misunderstood. While growing up, I had heard that term, but I never knew what it meant. This term isn't considered a diagnosis by the mental health authorities. Instead, it's a loose term created to describe several conditions a person might be experiencing. For example, a person might be experiencing a panic attack or a nervous attack, depression, or insomnia; they might have difficulty focusing on and completing a task; they might be experiencing unusual fatigue or brain fog. All of these are symptoms of what we call a nervous breakdown.

Many mental health experts define a nervous breakdown as *a debilitating state of stress where an individual is incapable of doing simple tasks.* So the things that were once easy for you have become difficult and nearly impossible for you to do because of stress. Your ability to focus is impaired. Your body has shut down, making it impossible for you to do anything; this is where I found myself.

Growing up, I could never have imagined experiencing a nervous breakdown. But this is not as uncommon as some might think. Millions of people go through this every day without knowing it. They overwork themselves, giving themselves no time to rest. They overthink situations and keep their stress levels high, thereby thrusting their bodies into a constant state of fight-or-flight—this keeps continuous pressure on their bodies until their bodies eventually shut down from exhaustion. It's all right to experience stress at certain times, but to remain in a state of stress for long periods with no break is very unhealthy, even deadly. And this is why so many Americans are experiencing mental health problems; this is why there is such a mental health crisis in our society today. Everyone is overworked and stressed out, and very few people are resting. So many people are in a rat race to become successful in life; they're workaholics who don't know how to relax and enjoy life, enjoy the little things and appreciate every moment. They neglect their families for money, neglect God to focus on their careers, and even neglect their health just to focus on their careers. As one person put it: *You spend*

CHAPTER 4: A DARK STATE OF MIND

all of your health trying to get wealth and then spend all of your wealth trying to regain your health. That pretty much sums it up.

I can understand what people are going through when they talk about having a mental health crisis. I experienced one. I'd heard of people losing it, going crazy, and snapping out of nowhere. I'd heard of people going from living a regular life to living in a mental institution, some wandering the streets as if lost and confused, looking like zombies. But for me to go from hearing about it to experiencing these things was surreal. And it's difficult for me to explain to many people.

MY EXPERIENCE

It happened out of the blue one day. I was leaving a meeting with my daughter's teacher at her school—her grades were terrible. My stress level skyrocketed. I didn't know what to do. She was brilliant but not focused. She allowed her grades to slip and put herself further and further behind in her classwork. Like any parent, my concern was for my daughter's future. I worried that she might make bad decisions like I did coming up; it is not a good sign when grades drop. Satan magnified the situation and darkened my thinking; I could only think of the worst possible outcomes.

I had underestimated the toll stress was taking on me. You see, I didn't want to listen to my body. Furthermore, I didn't want to listen to God. So I tried to play God and solve all of my problems myself. Taking this on myself, I did not realize I was placing even more stress on my already overstressed mind. My daughter's school situation was just another problem on top of the many issues I was already dealing with in my life, not to mention all of the other unresolved issues I had never dealt with from my childhood. I believed at that time that I'd made a huge mess of my life:

- A criminal record that followed me everywhere I went.
- A bad reputation.
- Relationship problems that left me feeling empty and emotionally depleted.

A simple three-minute walk from that classroom to my car in the parking lot seemed like an eternity as my body began to feel weaker and weaker. With each step, I felt all of my strength fleeing; it was like my legs were trapped in quicksand or had cinderblocks on them. My head began to spin as if dizzy, my sight growing blurry. I desperately needed to sit down, or I knew I would have passed out on the pavement. As I got closer to my car, I heard a voice say in my head, "You are about to have a nervous breakdown."

The worse part of this whole ordeal was the complete feeling of helplessness, the loss of control over my body. I was not in control. I couldn't stop what was happening to me. All I could do was watch my body shut down and feel the tremors permeating my nervous system like the shaking of an earthquake. Cold chills took over my body as fear took hold of my soul. I was now in a pit of mental darkness. I was cracking up mentally and falling to pieces right in that parking lot.

I wouldn't have been any good for my children if I'd

CHAPTER 4: A DARK STATE OF MIND

completely lost it. Truthfully, if I had completely lost it, I wouldn't have been any good for myself. That incident taught me an important lesson: my mental health is valuable, and I must protect it at all costs. Nothing in this world is worth losing your mind over. Nothing! If you lose a business, you can start one again. If you lose a house, you can buy another. If you lose a car, you can purchase another one. If you lose a loved one, you can always fall back into the arms of the many loved ones you have left. If you lose a good opportunity, there will be others available. If you lose your job, there are plenty of other jobs available. If you destroy your name and reputation, you can always rebuild it. But if you lose your mind, that's it—you have nothing left. If your mental health is damaged, you can't rebuild, redeem, restructure, reorganize, or regain anything in life. I discovered that worry is more than a mental state; it is a sin. Fear and anxiety are tools of Satan used to keep us in a pit of darkness where our mental health is forever in jeopardy. The devil wants to destroy us mentally to devour every other aspect of our lives.

THE REAL BATTLEFIELD

Evangelist Joyce Meyers said it best: the mind is the battlefield. As Believers, we must remember that the enemy attacks us by firing the arrows of negative thoughts and beliefs into our minds to keep us discouraged and defeated. It is for this reason that the Apostle Paul wrote,

> "We are human, but we don't wage war as humans do. We use God's mighty weapons, not worldly weapons,

to knock down the strongholds of human reasoning and to destroy false arguments." (2 Corinthians 10:3-4, NLT)

The devil attacks our minds with lies about ourselves and God every day. He attacks our minds with negativity and wrong perceptions about our circumstances, trying to get us to see the glass as half-empty rather than half-full and getting us to feel as if our situations are hopeless rather than opportunities for God to show His strength and power. But, most of all, the devil is always trying to lock us in a cage of self-loathing and shame, making us feel as if we aren't good enough in this world, making us feel like we aren't deserving of God's blessings.

To be honest, no one is deserving of the blessings of God. No one has earned God's love and grace. No one can earn them. God's mercy and goodness are free gifts He gives us out of His love for us. God's salvation is a free gift He gives to us, and the way to receive this gift is to believe in Jesus by faith, acknowledge Him as your Lord and Savior, and believe that He died on the cross and rose from the grave on the third day (Romans 10:9).

Ephesians 2:8-9 says, "God saved you by his grace when you believed. And you can't take credit for this; it is a gift from God. Salvation is not a reward for the good things we have done, so none of us can boast about it" (NLT). Notice that? God doesn't want you feeling like you earned any of His blessings. Why? He doesn't want you to get caught up in yourself and develop the big-head (become arrogant). If you

CHAPTER 4: A DARK STATE OF MIND

were good enough to earn God's blessings, you'd be comparing yourself to other people and looking down upon them. Since the Bible declares that "all have sinned and fall short of the glory of God" (Romans 3:23) and your righteousness is like "filthy rags" in God's eyes (Isaiah 64:6), that means you have no other choice but to remain humble and realize that you're no better than anyone else in God's eyes. We are all sinners in need of God's grace and living off the mercy of God. The difference between a Believer and a sinner is that they acknowledge their dependence on God and choose to rely on God's power rather than their own. The Believer turns to God instead of turning to themselves and other things. The Believer relies on the Holy Spirit's power; for it is He who enables us to live right and do the right thing when our flesh wants to do the wrong thing; it is He who convicts us and corrects us when our flesh tries to steer us in the wrong direction.

You're in a place of darkness when you believe you can earn God's blessings; this is what is known as spiritual deception. You'll always fall short when trying to be righteous. And when you fall short and mess up, the devil will always be there to shame you; he will always be there to remind you of your mistakes and communicate to you how unworthy you are in life. But for the Believer who knows God's Word and walks in His light, they know how to remind Satan of God's Word—they'll let the devil know they're not worthy, but Christ made them worthy that day He shed His blood on the cross and took our sins upon His shoulders. We can remind the devil that we are operating in the righteousness of Christ, and not our own, and that Christ has redeemed us from the penalty of sin and washed us clean with His blood. We can remind Satan that we have been made brand new creations in Christ Jesus and that all of the blessings of God outlined in the Word of God is ours for the taking because Christ made them available to us by faith. We don't have to earn a blessing because Jesus earned the blessings of the Father for us on the cross.

Sure, we mess up, but that's why God gave us His Spirit. The Holy Spirit helps us get up and brush ourselves off every time we fall. We grow from our mistakes rather than get buried and crushed by them. Adversity strengthens our faith rather than shaming us. As the Bible puts it, "And we know that God causes everything to work together for the good of those who love God and are called according to his purpose for them" (Romans 8:28, NLT). So even the bad things are working for our good; therefore, we can rejoice even when things don't go our way. As a Believer, when you lose a job, that's because a better one is waiting for you. When you lose a house, that's because a better one is up the road. When people reject you, it's because God is protecting you from the wrong crowd. In all things, you can rejoice!

God works better through our weaknesses. The Bible tells us that. The Apostle Paul said,

> "Each time he said, 'My grace is all you need. My power works best in weakness.' So now I am glad to boast about my weaknesses, so that the power of Christ can work through me" (2 Corinthians 12:9, NLT).

God will allow us to fall weak so that we can turn to Him for

CHAPTER 4: A DARK STATE OF MIND

strength. He will let us exhaust ourselves to the point where we run out of strength and energy and have no other choice but to look to Him for strength and the energy to get through the day. God has grace stored up for each new day in our lives, but we have to seek Him before doing anything. Psalm 68:19 says, "Blessed be the Lord, who daily loadeth us with benefits, even the God of our salvation. Selah." In the New International Version (NIV) translation, that verse reads, "Praise be to the Lord, to God our Savior, who daily bears our burdens." Daily, God has new blessings in store for us, and He wants to take our burdens upon Himself. He wants to help us and bless us...daily! God never gets tired of seeing your face and hearing your voice; He doesn't get tired of helping you. There's no such thing as outwearing your welcome when it comes to God. He sits back and waits for you each day to go to Him and ask for His help. Why? Your problems are the opportunities He needs to demonstrate how real He is on this earth. Or, as the Bible puts it in 2 Chronicles 16:9, "For the eyes of the LORD run to and fro throughout the whole earth, to shew himself strong in the behalf of them whose heart is perfect toward him."

    It took me nearly losing my mind before I discovered what I'm sharing with you. God had to let me fall and hit rock bottom before I learned to call upon Him in prayer and let Him take control of my life. He wanted me to stop trying to figure things out and take everything to Him in prayer, releasing all of my burdens into His hands and trusting by faith that He would work them out on His own. He didn't need my help; He just needed my cooperation. God is the One with the wisdom to know what needs to be done and has the power to do it. He has all of the power in His hands; I did not. The only thing God had to do in my life was destroy the many wrong beliefs (strongholds) I held about Him and life so that I could fully surrender to Him.

Even though I'd accepted Christ as my Lord and Savior and even turned to Him while in prison, I still held onto certain beliefs that were making it difficult for God to work in my life as He intended. Not only that, but I was still opening doors for the demonic to operate in my mind. I know plenty of people believe a Believer can't have a demon operating in their life, but I haven't found any Scriptures to support that claim. On the contrary, 1 Peter 1:14 says, "[Live] as obedient children [of God]; do not be conformed to the evil desires which governed you in your ignorance [before you knew the requirements and transforming power of the good news regarding salvation]" (Amplified Bible). Whenever you walk in darkness (which means ignorance of the Word of God), you leave yourself open to the deceptions of demons. For this very reason, the Bible warns us in 2 Corinthians 2:11, "Lest Satan should get an advantage of us: for we are not ignorant of his devices." The devil can trick Believers who don't know God's Word and operate in spiritual ignorance.

On that note, I want to highlight another form of darkness many people find themselves trapped in due to ignorance: the occult.

CHAPTER 4: A DARK STATE OF MIND

Meditation Verses

"'Don't copy the behavior and customs of this world, but let God transform you into a new person by changing the way you think. Then you will learn to know God's will for you, which is good and pleasing and perfect." (Romans 12:2, NLT)

"For, who can know the LORD's thoughts? Who knows enough to teach him?" But we understand these things, for we have the mind of Christ." (1 Corinthians 2:16, NLT)

"There is no fear in love; but perfect love casteth out fear: because fear hath torment. He that feareth is not made perfect in love." (1 John 4:18)

"Don't worry about anything; instead, pray about everything. Tell God what you need, and thank him for all he has done." (Philippians 4:6, NLT)

Prayer

Dear Heavenly Father, I thank you for setting me free from every tormenting thought. I surrender my mind to you and accept your thoughts, peace and wisdom. Today, I cast down every demonic, negative thought and replace them with your word and promises. The blood of Jesus now covers my mind and I have the mind of Christ, in Jesus' name. Amen.

BLACKOUT

Chapter 5

INVITING EVIL

> "Wherefore come out from among them, and be ye separate, saith the Lord, and touch not the unclean thing; and I will receive you, And will be a Father unto you, and ye shall be my sons and daughters, saith the Lord Almighty."
> —2 Corinthians 6:17-18

As I share my story of blackouts, spouts of uncontrollable rage, wrestling with anger issues, and deep trauma, I must mention to you there is a spiritual component in all of this. I wasn't just dealing with the natural causes behind my anger and destructive behavior; I also dealt with the spiritual causes.

This is a very overlooked aspect of the mental health issue, and here's why: the scientific community at large doesn't recognize and acknowledge the existence of the spirit realm. They don't acknowledge the existence of God, Satan, angels and demons. They view things like demonic possession as some natural phenomenon that has a rational explanation that has yet to be discovered. They believe the only things that truly exist in this world are the things that appeal to our natural senses, and since the spirit world doesn't appeal to our natural senses, scientists disregard it as nonexistent.

The medical community and scientific communities work hand-in-hand; therefore, you won't find too many medical practitioners prescribing deliverance from demonic possession to deal with irrational behavior. Likewise, you're unlikely to find a medical doctor urging you to turn to God in prayer for healing.

Now, God uses doctors. The writer of the Gospel of Luke was a physician. In fact, Luke became the Apostle Paul's primary care physician. He prescribed Paul medicine to help with his eyesight. And yet, Luke was a powerful man of God, a Believer who depended on God's supernatural power and guidance in his life. Luke realized that there was only so much that medical science could do. He realized that Jesus was the great physician, doing that which the most skilled doctors couldn't do. Jesus was healing the sick and raising the dead, things that defied medical science and scientific explanation. The miracles of Christ were well documented throughout the Roman world by Roman historians like Josephus and Tacitus, not just by the Gospels' writers. So it was well known and established throughout the ancient world that Jesus was a miracle worker and that there was a power that was higher than man's available to us through prayer.

But fast forward. Today's scientists have set out to wage war against God and the Bible. For some strange reason, they want to replace God. They've replaced God with evolution in

CHAPTER 5: INVITING EVIL

the schools, replaced biblical morality with liberal philosophy in society, and now they want to squeeze out the little bit of God left in our hearts and minds. They want to tell us there is no afterlife, spiritual reality, God and devil, and hence, no supernatural power. But we all know that's not true. Countless supernatural experiences are being reported daily by everyday people. People are experiencing ghosts, being bitten and scratched by invisible entities, hearing invisible entities talk to them, and more. Unfortunately, when scientists receive these reports, they simply label them "paranormal" and brush them off to the side; they don't know what else to do with them.

Reports reveal that the youth are turning to witchcraft more than any other religion in our society today. And yes, witchcraft is a religion; it's known as Wicca. There are more youth turning to and practicing Wicca today than ever before in our world. They're being introduced to this through movies and music. Movies like *Harry Potter* and *The Craft* have inspired young people at an alarming rate to pick up books of spells and magic wands, hoping to experience the supernatural in their own lives like the characters on the television screen. But this didn't just start today; it's been going on for a long time. Television shows like *Bewitched* and *The Adams Family* strongly promoted this theme, and later shows like *Sabrina The Teenage Witch*, *Charmed* and *Buffy The Vampire Slayer* took things a little bit further. Cartoons like *Pokemon* and *Dragon Ball Z* hooked little kids and introduced them to the world of magic and occultism. And today, it's nearly impossible to find a television station that's not promoting the occult. It's everywhere. And what people don't realize is they're inviting evil into their lives as they entertain and practice these things.

A DIVINE WARNING

Early on, God warned the Israelites not to practice the occult practices that fill our world today. For example, God told His people in Deuteronomy 18:9-12,

> "When you enter the land the LORD your God is giving you, be very careful not to imitate the detestable customs of the nations living there. For example, never sacrifice your son or daughter as a burnt offering. And do not let your people practice fortune-telling, or use sorcery, or interpret omens, or engage in witchcraft, or cast spells, or function as mediums or psychics, or call forth the spirits of the dead. Anyone who does these things is detestable to the LORD. It is because the other nations have done these detestable things that the LORD your God will drive them out ahead of you."

Notice what God called detestable ("deserving intense dislike"): human sacrifices; soothsaying (psychic fortunetelling); sorcery (in the Hebrew, this word is translated *kāšap*, and it literally means "to use or practice witchcraft"); things like the horoscopes and other tools of divination that are used to predict the future; spiritism, which is where a person tries to make contact with the spirit world for guidance; and necromancy, which is where one tries to communicate with the dead. God said anyone who does these things will incur His

CHAPTER 5: INVITING EVIL

wrath and judgment.

Why are these practices bad for us according to God? It's because they open doors into our lives to demonic spirits (or what the Bible calls "familiar spirits"). The Bible calls demons familiar spirits because they love to masquerade as that which is familiar to us. For example, they will pretend to be that dead aunt or uncle, parent or sibling, or historical figure you want to talk to and see. Demons love to trick us into thinking we are communicating with the spirits of the dead when in reality, we are communicating with demonic spirits.

The Bible says to be absent from the body for a Believer is to be present with the Lord (2 Corinthians 5:8). All that's saying is once our spirits exit our bodies, they either go with God in Heaven or go straight into a pit in Hell. Either way, our spirits don't linger around. So that ghost you're seeing isn't the spirit of some human being; it's a demonic spirit masquerading as a human's spirit. That's why so many people who encounter these ghosts report how sinister they are and how they'll usually change their appearances, becoming more grotesque and menacing at times. These are demons.

In ancient times, God warned His people to avoid praying to idols. Some people might not see this as dangerous—after all, an idol was just a piece of wood or stone fashioned in the image of a creature or god. So how could a piece of wood or stone harm anyone? Well, God let the Israelites know these idols were more than mere wood or stone; they were representations of demons. He said in Deuteronomy 32:16-17, "They stirred up his jealousy by worshiping foreign gods; they provoked his fury with detestable deeds. They offered sacrifices to demons, which are not God, to gods they had not known before, to new gods only recently arrived, to gods their ancestors had never feared" (NLT). Notice here that God called those wooden, stone statues demons. The structures weren't alive, but the entities they represented were alive and would become actively involved in the lives of those worshipping their images. When you reach out to demons, they will reach out to you. I discovered this early in my life when I plummeted into the world of the occult and unwittingly invited evil into my world.

THE SLUMBER PARTY

During my freshman year of high school, I remember inviting a couple of girls to my house for a slumber party. Of course, I had slumber parties before, so I knew that they could get boring and stale if you didn't do something fun or exciting. My goal was to make this one interesting, so I brought out an Ouija board. Now, even witches will tell you that these devices are dangerous. And to be blunt, all witchcraft, both black and white magic, is considered evil in the sight of God. But you know you're in serious trouble when witches begin warning you not to play with something that can introduce great evil.

Ouija boards are some of the most popular items used in occult-based films and shows. Undoubtedly, many children are introduced to these things through television. From there, they introduce them to their friends in settings like the one I was in. Ouija boards are a strong tool used to communicate with spirits. In the real-life case of *The Exorcist*, the child who became demon-possessed did so after playing with an Oui-

CHAPTER 5: INVITING EVIL

ja board. As a result, he released a presence in his home that caused considerable damage to him and his family. The movie *The Exorcist* was based on his life. And there are countless other tales like this.

My little sister was the one who brought the Ouija board home; a friend of hers gave it to her. When she first brought it home, my sisters and I played with it, trying to get it to work. That's when our mother walked in and discovered what we were doing. Mom told us to get that thing out of her house immediately, but we disobeyed her and kept it. We were unclear why she was so adamant about getting the Ouija board out of her house. Had she told us about the dangers of such a board, we probably would have complied.

We couldn't see how the board was harmful, especially since it was purchased at Toys-R-Us. In our minds, if that board was being sold inside of a children's store, then it had to be harmless. Also, it didn't require any batteries, and there weren't many instructions to follow. So we were lost about what to do to get the thing to work. But after a couple of hours of tampering with it, we finally figured out how to get it to work: we just had to believe. Belief was the secret ingredient to getting the planchette to move independently. And when that planchette moved, we were in total shock and disbelief about the talking game board. The plastic planchette was moving on its own. It took a few of our fingers to be rested lightly on the planchette as it glided across letters and numbers as if something from *the other side* was trying to send us a message. The excitement of that experience stuck with us and compelled us to bring my friends on board.

THE EXORCISM OF TESHAUNA

As I explained earlier in this book, I would often hear a voice telling me to do wrong. A voice would tell me to do evil and convince me that God wasn't watching what I did. I would hear voices telling me what to say to others to curse them out and even encouraging me not to let little things slip. I was being influenced by something evil without a shadow of a doubt. That evil is what placed my feet on the path of destruction. But I discovered that the devil doesn't show his true colors in our lives until we seek to part ways with him; that's when he will throw all Hell at us. For me, it happened the day I first surrendered my life to Christ. The day I called it quits on Satan was the day he showed his ugly face.

At first, it was like a scene out of a horror movie. I'd grown tired of my relationship with darkness. The devil was domineering, taking control of my life more and more. His goal was to consume me and destroy me from within completely. My mind was under extreme attack, and the enemy was leading me to believe I had done so much wrong that God would not accept me into His Kingdom, and any day soon, God was going to end my life. So I met with my pastor and turned my life over to Christ; after that, things got weird. First, Satan tried to convince me that the prayer of salvation I'd just prayed was done in vain. *Those were just empty words,* he uttered in my spirit. *What's the big deal?* I knew what the "big deal" was. When I prayed that prayer of surrender to God, I had tears flowing down my eyes; I believed them with all my heart and uttered them in total sincerity. I knew God

CHAPTER 5: INVITING EVIL

had heard my prayer.

After Satan failed to convince me to walk away from God, he began attacking me at night while sleeping. One night, I felt something physically holding me down in the bed, but no one was there. When I opened my eyes, I saw what looked like a black mass; it was hovering above me at first, but then it attempted to enter my body. I tried to lift my hands to fight it off, but I couldn't move my hands. It felt like something was holding my arms down to my sides like I was in a straight jacket. I tried to turn my head, but I couldn't. It was like something was holding my head still.

Furthermore, I couldn't open my mouth and utter a word. It was like my voice was gone; my ability to speak was suspended. I was terrified, not knowing what was going on or what to do. But after a moment, I felt a tap on the top of my head; it was as if the Holy Spirit was speaking to me and telling me what to do. At that moment, it dawned on me: Say the name of Jesus! But I couldn't open my mouth and say the name of Jesus. I couldn't scream, talk, yell, or anything. But then, the thought came to my mind to say the name of Jesus in my head. And so I did. When I began saying the name of Jesus in my mind, suddenly, the attack stopped. Whatever was holding me down in the bed lifted and went away. Suddenly, I could talk again. From that moment, I realized I was dealing with a real phenomenon. The spirit world is real. Demons are real. The battle we find ourselves in from day to day is a spiritual battle. You can't fight spirits with your fist; you have to fight them with the name and blood of Jesus. Demons recognize the authority of that name.

After that spirit lifted off of me, I immediately fell to my knees and began crying out to God. I didn't want that spirit to return and attack me anymore. That was singlehandedly the scariest thing I'd ever experienced in my life. Now, I wish I could tell you everything stopped that night I cried out to God, but it didn't. Off and on, I would experience similar spiritual attacks. But unlike the first time, I knew how to fight the enemy when he came. I would use the name of Jesus and then sense the spirit leave. Some nights I would be asleep when the enemy would attack. I would simply wake up and rebuke that spirit in the name of Jesus and then fall right back to sleep. After a while, the devil got the message and realized I would not give in, so he stopped attacking me that way.

Whenever you're in the dark about who you are as a Believer and the authority God has given you, the devil will mess with you and dominate over you. He's counting on you being ignorant of your authority in Christ. It's not holy water, physical crosses, statues of Mary and the baby Jesus, cards, and rosary beads that give us power over demons; it is the name of Jesus that makes demons flee. Furthermore, our understanding of our true identities in Christ makes Satan's knees buckle. To better illustrate this, I remember one night when the devil attacked me. I could hear in my spirit what sounded like troops getting ready to go into battle. I could feel the weight of darkness around me. This time, I could sense in my spirit that God wanted me to do more than just say the name of Jesus to end this attack; He wanted me to let the enemy know that I knew who I was in Christ also. So when the enemy began to attack me, I heard the Spirit of God

CHAPTER 5: INVITING EVIL

coaching me on what to say to the enemy. I began to say, "I am a child of God! Greater is He that is in me than He that is in the world! I am not alone! God is with me!" And as I spoke truth to the power of darkness, I could feel the light of God pushing back the darkness that was surrounding me and trying to take over my mind. As I later learned, God was training me how to fight in the spirit.

We're in a spiritual war. It's important that we learn how to fight in the spirit. The weapons God has given us to fight the enemy are the Word of God, the name of Jesus, and the blood of Jesus. God has placed His anointing on us as Believers, but He has also given us the power to tread on the heads of demons in Jesus' name (Luke 10:19). God

God has given us power over Satan, but we have to use that power. Furthermore, we have to shut every doorway we've opened to the devil through ignorance and the occult.

SHUT THE DOOR
The Bible declares in 2 Corinthians 6:14-17,

> "'Do not be yoked together with unbelievers. For what do righteousness and wickedness have in common? Or what fellowship can light have with darkness? What harmony is there between Christ and Belial? Or what does a believer have in common with an unbeliever? What agreement is there between the temple of God and idols? For we are the temple of the living God. As God has said: 'I will live with them and walk among them, and I will be their God, and they will be

my people.' Therefore, 'Come out from them and be separate, says the Lord. Touch no unclean thing, and I will receive you.'" (NIV)

Demons enter into our lives through open doors (opportunities we give them due to our disobedience towards God and our involvement with demonic activities and objects). Joining occult groups and playing with mysterious objects invites demons. Becoming a part of circles where people pray to idol gods, and communicate with demons will open you to demonic activity. And when demons enter your world, they'll try to take over your home and afflict your family. But getting rid of the enemy in your life is simple. First, you must surrender your life to Christ and allow Him to become your Lord and Savior. Second, you must denounce the works of darkness and break the covenant with demons. To do so, pray this prayer after me:

> Lord Jesus, I surrender my life to you today. I receive you as my Lord and Savior. Come into my heart and be my Lord and Savior. Wash me with your blood and make me the person you created me to be. I am yours. My mind is yours. My body is yours; it is the property of the Most High God. Therefore, I denounce all attachments and covenants I've made with the kingdom of darkness, demons, and Satan. I cancel every contract I've made with the enemy that gave him legal rights to my body, home, and family. Today, I destroy every agreement with the enemy

CHAPTER 5: INVITING EVIL

and declare that whom God has set free are free indeed. I am a new creation in Christ Jesus today. I no longer belong to the enemy.

Therefore, Satan, you no longer have the legal right to touch my body, my family, and operate in my household. You are defeated, and the blood of Jesus is against you. My body is now the temple of the Holy Spirit. Every demonic affliction against my body and mind, sickness and disease, an attack against my health, finances, and progress is defeated. Everything the devil stole from me, he must give it back seven-fold. I declare that the angels of the Lord are camped all around me, and my household and no weapon formed against me shall prosper. I declare this in Jesus' name, amen.

Now, suppose you have any occult objects in your house (crystals, Ouija boards, idols, books of spells and incantations, occultic oils, and incense such as sage and other tools of the occult, books of horoscopes, movies, and demonic music). In that case, the next step is for you to get a large trash bag and throw these things away. Get them out of your house and life, and watch how the presence of the Lord will fill the atmosphere.

In the next chapter, I will highlight a dangerous idol all of us must dethrone if we're to allow God to take control of our lives.

Meditation Verses

"'When you enter the land the LORD your God is giving you, be very careful not to imitate the detestable customs of the nations living there. For example, never sacrifice your son or daughter as a burnt offering. And do not let your people practice fortune-telling, or use sorcery, or interpret omens, or engage in witchcraft, or cast spells, or function as mediums or psychics, or call forth the spirits of the dead. Anyone who does these things is detestable to the LORD. It is because the other nations have done these detestable things that the LORD your God will drive them out ahead of you." (Deuteronomy 18:9-12, NLT)

"Many who became believers confessed their sinful practices. A number of them who had been practicing sorcery brought their incantation books and burned them at a public bonfire. The value of the books was several million dollars. So the message about the Lord spread widely and had a powerful effect." (Acts 19:18-20, NLT)

Prayer

Dear Heavenly Father, I repent of any and all involvement with the occult and witchcraft. I denouce all ties to witchcraft and cancel all contracts I've made with demons. I shut every open door to the enemy in my life. I plead the blood of Jesus over my life in Jesus' name. Amen.

Chapter 6

DETHRONING THE IDOL OF SELF

"So put to death the sinful, earthly things lurking within you. Have nothing to do with sexual immorality, impurity, lust, and evil desires. Don't be greedy, for a greedy person is an idolater, worshiping the things of this world."
—Proverbs 4:23, NLT

IN THE LAST CHAPTER, WE TALKED ABOUT THE dangers of occult objects. However, in this chapter, we need to address one of the biggest idols that tend to open the door to demonic activity in our lives and cause us to live wrongly. I want to talk about the idol of self. I know that might not seem like an idol to some people, but trust me when I tell you, we can become our biggest idols. Sometimes, it's not outside circumstances hindering us; it's our attitudes hindering us. Sometimes, it's not even the devil who's messing us up; our pride is destroying us and robbing us of God's blessings.

So what do I mean when I talk about the idol of self? Let me explain. When I talk about self, I'm talking about our stubborn insistence on having things our way. I'm talking about our unwillingness to submit to God and live life His way. I'm talking about our selfish, ego-driven, self-centered attitudes where we think life is about us, where we are more focused on satisfying and pleasing ourselves than living to serve and please God. Every day, we can have the option to either submit to God and follow His Spirit or submit to our flesh and follow its will.

The Bible talks about the flesh in Galatians 5:16-25. It says,

> "So I say, walk by the Spirit, and you will not gratify the desires of the flesh. For the flesh desires what is contrary to the Spirit, and the Spirit what is contrary to the flesh. They are in conflict with each other, so that you are not to do whatever you want. But if you are led by the Spirit, you are not under the law. The acts of the flesh are obvious: sexual immorality, impurity, and debauchery; idolatry and witchcraft; hatred, discord, jealousy, fits of rage, selfish ambition, dissensions, factions, and envy; drunkenness, orgies, and the like. I warn you, as I did before, that those who live like this will not inherit the kingdom of God. But the fruit of the Spirit is love, joy, peace, forbearance, kindness, goodness, faithfulness, gentleness and self-control. Against such things there is no law. Those who belong to Christ Jesus have crucified the flesh with its

CHAPTER 6: DETHRONING THE IDOL OF SELF

passions and desires. Since we live by the Spirit, let us keep in step with the Spirit." (NIV)

When the Bible talks about the flesh, it's referring to man's sinful nature. After the fall of man in the Garden of Eden, sin crept into the world and contaminated the earth and man's nature. So now, our natural tendency is to go in the opposite direction of God and do the opposite of His will. As Paul said, the flesh desires that which is "contrary" to God's Spirit. Human nature naturally wants to defy God. This is why the Bible says, "Behold, I was shapen in iniquity; and in sin did my mother conceive me" (Psalm 51:5). We came into this world with the sin nature, and throughout our lives we are taught how to live disobediently towards God. This is also why the Bible says, "For I know that in me (that is, in my flesh,) dwelleth no good thing: for to will is present with me; but how to perform that which is good I find not" (Romans 7:18).

In Matthew 19:16-17, the Bible says, "And, behold, one came and said unto him, Good Master, what good thing shall I do, that I may have eternal life? And he said unto him, Why callest thou me good? There is none good but one, that is, God: but if thou wilt enter into life, keep the commandments." Notice that Jesus quickly dismissed the idea that human nature can be "good" and redirected the young man's focus to God's standards (Commandments). Only God is good—that's the point Jesus was making. There's nothing "good" that we can do to get God's attention and impress Him. The only thing good in this world and universe is God and His righteous standards found in His Word.

You have a sinful nature, and so do I; however, we can either choose to give in to our sinful natures or submit to God's Spirit. As Paul emphasized, "Walk by the Spirit, and you will not gratify the desires of the flesh." We have the right as Believers to submit to God and starve the will of the flesh. Remember: whatever we feed the most, that's what will grow in our lives. Like Paul said, "Do not be deceived: God cannot be mocked. A man reaps what he sows. Whoever sows to please their flesh, from the flesh will reap destruction; whoever sows to please the Spirit, from the Spirit will reap eternal life" (Galatians 6:7-8, NIV). When we spend more time catering to our flesh, watching things, and listening to things that promote sinful cravings and lusts, then we're weakening our spirits and giving our sinful natures more power over us. If we spend more time reading God's Word, seeking His face and tuning our eyes and ears to the things that glorify God and build us up spiritually, we strengthen our spirits and gain power over the flesh. The flesh will always have its temptations, but we'll have the strength to say no to these temptations because we've built up our spiritual muscles. It's about what you invest your time in the most.

A SELFISH NATURE

As a child, no one had to teach me how to do wrong; it was in my nature. When I was four years old, I remember going to a department store with my mom. While there, I saw a blue bag with several compartments with different items. I wanted that bag, so I went to my mom and asked her if I could have it. She said no. That didn't sit well with me, so I took the bag.

CHAPTER 6: DETHRONING THE IDOL OF SELF

No one taught me how to steal; I just knew. I didn't get far, though. The store's alarm sounded off at the entrance. My mom noticed that I had the bag on me, attempting to steal it. She made me return it. Unfortunately, that wasn't the last time I stole something. As I got older, I continued to steal things. I would also desire to steal even when I had money to purchase what I wanted.

When I was six years old, I remember taking a yellow crayon and writing it all over the walls. At the time, I didn't think the yellow would show up as clearly as it did, but I was wrong—those markings were very visible. When my dad saw those markings, he was livid. The funny thing is I was walking with him when he discovered the marks, and not once did I admit that I marked up his walls. I didn't say anything either when he threatened to whoop my older sister and cousin if no one confessed to the act. I sat back quietly while watching my sister and cousin get whooped, and then I eventually went by then my dad was out of steam. The funny thing is no one had to teach me how to lie; it was just in me. To this day, my cousin will remind me of that incident from time to time. And how could I forget it? I let them get punished for something I did.

As I got older, I continued to walk in darkness, making an idol out of myself. As a young woman, I entered into this Ms. Independent phase where I felt like I didn't need anyone else, especially a man. Now, God didn't design anyone to be an island unto him or herself, but we also understand that God didn't create us to depend on others as our source either. We are to maintain a healthy, balanced approach, realizing that while God is the only person we truly need in life, He does work through people. So no one is totally independent. God uses people to bless us, help us, and even guide us. Money doesn't grow on trees; it comes from people's hands. When feeling sick, God has given us doctors to help us get well. God has given us counselors to guide us when in need of guidance. In fact, the Bible says on more than one occasion that when we make plans without first seeking wise counsel, our plans will ultimately fail (Proverbs 11:4, 15:22, 20:18; Psalm 1). It was God who said in Genesis 2:18 that it is not good for a man to be alone. We all need other people. But I'd gotten into my selfish mode, building a wall in my soul to protect me from further hurt from people, especially men. I was tired of hearing the same old lies and lines, being disrespected, taken advantage of. So I began to take myself out, seeking to know myself. And again, there's nothing wrong with that, but there is a problem when we allow bitterness and hurt to become the driving force behind our actions, and we close our hearts to others.

I declared that the only three people I needed were me, myself, and I, enabling me to live selfishly; it also provided me with the entitlement to be rude to others, which isn't good. I would lift the bar too high for others to reach just to be with me and often seek to remain alone so I didn't have to feel accountable to others. I was living in a bubble and blaming everyone else for my misery. I was lying to myself. That's what pride and bitterness will cause us to do to ourselves.

I was out of control, running up credit cards and racking up debt because I wanted to live for myself rather than

CHAPTER 6: DETHRONING THE IDOL OF SELF

God. It was all about me and what I wanted, and if I couldn't have something, I would sit back and figure out a way to get it without ever stopping to ask if it was God's will for me to have it or if it belonged to someone else. I listened to impulses rather than wisdom. I wrote checks I couldn't cash and racked up fees, ruining my name. I ended up filing for bankruptcy twice. I refused to be a good steward of the money God gave me.

    I was reckless and out of control even when it came to my health; it was like I didn't care if I lived or died. I remember eating foods I knew I was allergic to in one incident. I'm allergic to shrimp, but I can eat crab and lobster as long as I don't mix alcohol with my consumption of these foods. However, I recall going out to dinner and then going to the bar and having an alcoholic beverage. I forgot that was a dangerous combination! *What was I thinking?* I didn't take my life seriously at the time. It wasn't long before my ears started tingling and itching, and my throat began to close up, shutting off my airway passage. I took some Benadryl because I did not have an EpiPen, but it wasn't working. I didn't have time to find my friend, to tell her what was happening because every second counted for me to obtain medical treatment. I was playing Russian Roulette with my life; instead of bullets, I used food and alcohol. Only God's grace allowed me to remain coherent and conscious enough to drive myself to the nearest hospital and receive help. I made it to the desk while feeling like I was about to pass out. And I did because I don't remember much of anything that happened after making it to that desk. I can vaguely recall hearing the voices of little children telling me to get up while nudging me with their feet. Yes, that was weird.

I was out of it. I do not know what my vital signs reflected, but it wasn't good. As I was gaining consciousness, I heard a nurse talking to another one, saying if I didn't respond, she was going to stick a tube down my throat. I learned that I had an anaphylactic shock, a rare severe allergic reaction that can be deadly if not treated right away.

Because of my careless actions, my children could have ended up motherless. I could have died. I'd been telling myself I needed to change my life, but I didn't know where to start or what to do. However, that incident really impressed upon me how fragile life is and just how quickly it can be snuffed out. When facing death, we tend to think more seriously about our lives and become more determined to do what it takes to live better lives.

Thankfully, God wasn't done with me yet. It was His grace and mercy that preserved me. In my spirit, I felt I wasn't alone, and I also realized that my recovery wasn't merely due to the efforts of the nurses and doctors but the supernatural power of God. I still had a purpose of fulfilling divine assignments to complete and more. Furthermore, I wasn't ready to die in my state—my heart was too full of anger, hate, and unforgiveness.

My selfishness made me feel entitled to express anger rather than resolve matters in a civilized manner. For example, I had episodes of road rage where I could have gotten seriously hurt or even killed. In one incident, I was driving, and a person was driving behind me with their high beam lights on. Every time I would switch lanes, they would change lanes too. I began to think they were following me. I then stopped my

CHAPTER 6: DETHRONING THE IDOL OF SELF

car, got out, walked over to that person's car, and confronted them. They could have been a serial killer, a psychopath, a rapist, or someone having a terrible day and wasn't in the mood for it; it didn't matter. I just wanted to do what I wanted to do despite the Holy Spirit's warning to stay in the car and just keep moving. After getting back in my car, the Holy Spirit convicted me even more about what I'd just done. I tried to justify my actions but couldn't. I was entirely wrong.

In another incident, my sons and I were at Outback Steakhouse. My boys had to go to the restroom. While in the restroom, an older man turned the lights off, leaving them in the dark. Perhaps it was a simple mistake, but that didn't matter to me. I was irate. My oldest son knew about my temper, but my youngest son didn't. So as my youngest son was telling me about what happened, my oldest son had a nervous look on his face. He sensed I was going to go and cause a scene by confronting the guy. And if it were not for the look on my son's face. That look convicted me and caused me to ask myself, *Teshauna, what are you doing?* I felt horrible that my son was embarrassed to be around me due to my behavior. After that, I began to look at myself and how my actions hurt those I loved.

In what was perhaps my most embarrassing moment, I remember getting into a fight with another lady while picking up my children from daycare. Daycare is supposed to be one of the safest environments for children, free from drama and fear. But not that day because I ran into the person who lied on me; it seemed like the perfect time to set the record straight. I wanted to prove a point. (This is just a side note not to get in someone else's business to defend a person when you know he/she is having an affair with someone else's husband/wife.) That was a habit of mine—I'd do whatever it took to clear my name if I felt like I was being lied on or disrespected. It was all about my image and not my integrity and character. Those children didn't need to be exposed to that; they didn't need to be traumatized by my actions all because of my ego. I wasn't thinking about them at the time. I didn't value my freedom, and I would fight without the fear of consequences. I would perceive the situation a certain way, now-triggered to fight when it wasn't necessary, thinking violence was the surest way for me to control others. I wanted to be feared. The truth is, I was just scared and used violence as a way to protect my heart. I was only concerned with myself. It wasn't until I got locked up that I realized how bad my anxiety and fear were and noticed that my temper was really a defense mechanism. And that is when I began to repent of anger, seeing it as a sin rather than just an emotion. I realized that the road rage I'd displayed was due to my unwillingness to cooperate and surrender to God. My fight at the daycare was due to my reluctance to submit to the Holy Spirit, who was telling me to pursue peace rather than violence. My outbursts of anger were based on selfishness and were not justified. Pride was driving my actions due to my stubbornness and rebellion against God. Pride is a sin. It is an insult against God, and this is why He hates a proud look.

THE ABORTION MILL

Being careless, young, and naive, I cared very little, if any,

CHAPTER 6: DETHRONING THE IDOL OF SELF

about the life of the unborn. I would get pregnant and then have an abortion without much thought of what I was doing. I did this so much; I remember one of my friends saying, "You can't keep doing that! Why do you decide not to keep the baby every time you get pregnant?" She earnestly tried to open my eyes to the reality of what I was doing to my body and the gift of life God placed inside me.

Abortion is not a form of birth control. And looking back, my acts of abortion weren't justified by any means. I didn't want to deal with the responsibility associated with having sex. I'd had one child out of wedlock and didn't want any more unless I was married. However, I didn't want to wait until I was married first to have sex. I started off doing things backwards, so it was easy to continue down the rebellious path of destruction. My marriage was rocky, and I refused to have more children and be stuck raising them by myself. And I was too prideful; I couldn't stand the idea of being embarrassed and talked about is when I decided to have my first abortion. It seemed easy to get rid of what I thought was a problem, just like sweeping up trash off the floor. Once divorced, I refused to have any more children, resulting in multiple baby daddies; I was too concerned with maintaining an image that never was the truth.

I remember dating one guy who told me he was infertile—he couldn't produce babies, and I believed him. We began having sex; afterwards, I discovered I was pregnant with his child, which angered me. And sadly, I barely knew the guy. I told him I was pregnant, which brought him great joy, but I wasn't willing to keep the baby. He begged and pleaded with me to keep the baby, even offering to take the baby and raise it by himself if necessary, but I was too selfish for that. I didn't care that the child deserved a shot at life and that this man desperately wanted his child to live; I just terminated the child. I wanted things to go my way, and I wasn't willing to bend.

The damage abortion does to the body and soul is immeasurable. Yes, abortion damages the mind and the psyche of the individual involved. You cannot shed innocent blood and continue with a clean conscience. Abortion providers will do everything in their power to convince you that abortions won't have any adverse psychological and physiological effects, but that's because they get paid handsomely for every abortion performed. It's in their financial interest to persuade you to go through with the abortion, but it's not worth its toll on your body and mind. I didn't understand that early on. I couldn't understand why so many people were protesting the abortion clinics and the practice of abortion. But I had a change of heart after seeing the movie *Unplanned*. This movie featured testimonies from different women, including a woman who was the youngest director of Planned Parenthood. She shared her reasons for leaving the organization. After seeing that movie, I felt so heartbroken; although I repented of my actions many years ago, I learned there were more layers to my healing that needed to take place in my life to be free from wearing the self-righteous cloak of shame.

The Holy Spirit revealed that I was blaming the men in my life for my abortions, even claiming they ruined my life. I still wasn't taking responsibility for my actions. I was angry, but at the wrong person. It wasn't the guys I should have been

CHAPTER 6: DETHRONING THE IDOL OF SELF

upset with, but I should've been upset with myself. Truthfully, the guys I was involved with were neutral or trying to talk me out of having the abortions. But I wanted to prove that I was in control of my life, living for myself. Instead, I was controlled by the idol of ego and made terrible decisions along the way, decisions that would cost me dearly up the road.

That movie opened my eyes. But, while watching it, the devil kept whispering in my spirit, that's not true. He did his best to dissuade me from the film's viewpoints and deter me from heading the conviction God was placing in my spirit. He tried his best to distract me from paying attention to the film, hoping I'd remain uninformed about the realities of abortion and the abortion industry, but I wasn't going to let him get the best of me. I wasn't going to fall for Satan's lies, not this time.

The devil is a master of deception. He knows that if we come into the knowledge of the truth, we'll stop putting up with his foolishness and falling for his lies. He, therefore, attempts to keep us blind and distracted so we won't pursue the truth. For example, each time I had a child, a simple glimpse at the ultrasounds would fill me with joy and excitement over the baby. However, the workers won't allow mothers to see their babies' ultrasounds at the Planned Parenthood clinics.

Now, if you've had an abortion, I don't want you to sulk in a pit of shame. The past is the past, and you can't go back in time to change it. God forgives, and when He forgives us, He tosses our sins into the sea of forgetfulness (Micah 7:19). So realize that Christ Jesus has set you free from the guilt and shame of your past; if this is you, forgive yourself, male or female, for whatever part you planned in killing an innocent life. But you need to be informed about the dangers of abortion and discontinue that activity. Life is a precious gift from God, and every baby is given to us by the Lord above. Babies are living beings created in the image and likeness of God, and they deserve a chance to live, even those forming in the womb. God sent them here for a purpose. They have a divine assignment on their lives, too. And call it what you want, but the Bible's term for abortion is murder. So repent, get up and commit to living life God's way.

*

Selfishness and self-centeredness are dangerous. The Bible says, "For rebellion is as the sin of witchcraft, and stubbornness is as iniquity and idolatry" (1 Samuel 15:23). Stubbornness is the same as idolatry, which is the act of worshipping another god besides God. Insisting on doing things and living life your way is a form of idolatry. Refusing to submit to God and His instructions because you want to satisfy and please yourself and live life on your terms is a form of idolatry. People today are redefining marriage, redefining sexuality, engaging in sexually immoral acts and all kinds of perversions, and justifying these things simply because they have chosen to make idols out of themselves. But remember that God will judge us for the sin of idolatry just as He did the Israelites and the Canaanites. So, if I were you, I'd cast down the idol of self real fast and decide that you're going to submit to God's Word even if your flesh doesn't want to. Let your flesh kick and scream, pout and protest all it wants; let God be the Lord

CHAPTER 6: DETHRONING THE IDOL OF SELF

of your life and choose to obey Him. And realize that your life is not your own; it belongs to the Lord (Proverbs 16).

Meditation Verses

"'Because of the privilege and authority God has given me, I give each of you this warning: Don't think you are better than you really are. Be honest in your evaluation of yourselves, measuring yourselves by the faith God has given us. (Romans 12:3, NLT)

"You shall have no other gods before me. You shall not make for yourself a carved image, or any likeness of anything that is in heaven above, or that is in the earth beneath, or that is in the water under the earth. You shall not bow down to them or serve them, for I the Lord your God am a jealous God, visiting the iniquity of the fathers on the children to the third and the fourth generation of those who hate me, but showing steadfast love to thousands of those who love me and keep my commandments. (Exodus 20:3-6, ESV)

Prayer

Dear Heavenly Father, I repent of idolatry. Forgive me for placing people, places and things before you and placing my confidence and trust in others. Forgive me for relying on my understanding rather than seeking your face. Today, I repent for every selfish act of adultery, fornication, abortion, lust, anger, and pride. I receive your humility and Spirit and thank you for your character, the Fruit of the Spirit, in my life today in Jesus' name. Amen.

Chapter 7

WALKING IN THE LIGHT

"For once you were full of darkness, but now you have light from the Lord. So live as people of light!"—Ephesians 5:8, NLT

I'D REDEDICATED MY LIFE TO CHRIST, AND WHEN I did, God showed me how messed up my life really was. He opened my eyes to the ugly truth about myself. As I mentioned earlier, I served the idol of self and allowed myself to be led by demonic spirits. But now, God was giving me the gift of discernment to recognize the voice behind the thoughts I was thinking. I realized that the voices telling me to do evil were demonic spirits. The enemy was using my pain to control me, and not only that, but he held me hostage to the darkness through a few of the habits and activities I was involved in. So one of the first things God began to convict me of when I fully surrendered my life to Him was my lifestyle choices.

BLACKOUT

A CHANGED HEART

One of the lifestyle choices I had to give up completely was hanging out in the bars, although I was going only a few times out of the month. It was the perfect environment for all hell to break loose and for me to get into trouble. The atmosphere is set up for you to escape your troubled life, but it gives you the illusion that everything will be all right. Unfortunately, alcohol and drugs will make matters worse for you and make life hard, especially if you're wrestling with deep emotional and psychological issues such as anger and trauma. Drugs and alcohol can turn you into a monster, causing you to say and do things you wouldn't normally do when you are in your right mind. And the inverse effect these substances will have on your life is that they will send your life spiraling out of control. Once your life becomes an even bigger mess due to these substances, you'll turn to these substances for an escape from the painful reality you have just created. This is a vicious cycle.

    God wanted me to escape the cycle I was in. He wanted me to break free from living a double life, which meant I had to change certain habits in my life, one being the places I would hang out. I had to stop hanging out at the bars and nightclubs. Those places were magnets for trouble in my life. Something simple as sitting at the bar and a lady spilling her drink on me could spark a brawl, or some chic stepping on my shoes or looking at me funny because they think I'm looking at their man. So again, the bar was the wrong place for someone like me; technically, it's the wrong place for anyone to be.

    God's transformation in your life begins with Him

CHAPTER 7: WALKING IN THE LIGHT

changing your heart's desires. Philippians 2:13 says, "For God is working in you, giving you the desire and the power to do what pleases him" (NLT). When God is changing you, you'll find yourself falling out of love with the things you used to love that are harmful to your soul, and you'll suddenly experience a desire to know God more and do that which pleases Him. For example, I fell out of love with the bars and clubs. I no longer found pleasure in them. When I would go, I felt empty and lost while in them. I would start to ask myself questions while there: *What am I looking for? I've been coming to this place year after year and still feel empty, so why am I still here?* My spirit began to hunger and thirst for true fulfillment. Like Jesus said to the woman at the well, if she would but drink of the Living water (which is Christ), she'll never thirst again (feel empty and unfulfilled).

The desires of your heart reveal the true condition of your heart. The Bible says, "Satan, who is the god of this world, has blinded the minds of those who don't believe. They are unable to see the glorious light of the Good News. They don't understand this message about the glory of Christ, who is the exact likeness of God" (2 Corinthians 4:4, NLT). Satan is a master at hiding the true condition of our hearts from us. We often believe we're on the right path when we're not. Proverbs 4:23 says, "Guard your heart above all else, for it determines the course of your life" (NLT). So, if our hearts are corrupt, our lives will be corrupt. If our hearts are out of alignment with God, our lives will be out of alignment with His will, and the worse part is we'll never know it.

Proverbs 16:2 tells us, "All the ways of a man are clean

in his own eyes; but the LORD weigheth the spirits." I like the way this verse reads in the New Living Translation (NLT): "People may be pure in their own eyes, but the LORD examines their motives." Everyone thinks their way is the right way, but only God can determine when we're off course in life. He knows the true condition of our hearts and where our lives are headed. And it's important to note that God doesn't send anyone into destruction; our hearts send us into destruction when they're filled with destructive desires and beliefs. That is why God first deals with our hearts, exposing our true motives, hidden intentions, and inner beliefs: He wants to change the direction of our lives and condition us to walk in His blessings.

The advertisement usually says, "Food and spirits"—that's so true. In the bar, that's just what you find: spirits. Alcohol brings a spirit you don't want to have, one that makes us do crazy things. And the food there may satisfy the hunger in your belly but not the hunger in your soul. I was hungry, but for the wrong things. It started to take me a long time to get ready to hang out at night, which meant I would leave the house later and later. I had so much energy for the bar, but that energy would leave as quickly as it came once there. I'd find myself leaving the bar at around 2 am. Even then, I would be hanging around talking, stopping to eat, spending money I didn't have on temporary fulfillment, depriving my body of rest, and going home to bed empty. Secretly, I was looking for love. I would go to the bars hoping to meet the man of my dreams. I had this fantasy of meeting the perfect man who would sweep me off my feet and take me away from my misery

CHAPTER 7: WALKING IN THE LIGHT

and pain. I would arrive with the expectation that this could be my lucky night.

There's always a motive behind our actions. There's a reason I would dress up in all of those fancy clothes—I wanted everyone's attention on me. I wanted people to focus on my looks instead of my inner pain. You could find me dancing, lifting my hands on the dance floor like I was in church worshiping God, drinking, and using foul language. I was planting seeds. But in the end, I had nothing to show for all of the offerings I gave Satan. I was suffocating internally.

When God began to reveal Himself to me, one of the first things He did was reveal to me the emptiness in my heart and the true motivations behind my actions. One of the hardest things to face was my mess. Seeing and accepting my motives was difficult. We like to deceive ourselves into thinking we are pure when we're not. We don't want to face the truth about ourselves. We often lie to ourselves to save face and feel superior to other people. But a slice of humble pie is required if we're going to change.

What I was looking for wasn't what I needed. I wanted a man and had stooped to the level of messing with married men, knowing they would never be honest with me. I'd tell myself his wife or girlfriend better not confront me, or they would get more than they were expecting.

I lowered my property value. My brother once said, "Teshauna, you can't lower your property value. Be careful who you allow into your life. Everybody is not worthy of your time." He was talking about standards. I wish I could say I maintained high standards, but I didn't. I began to let other people define me. I was like Dorothy from *The Wizard of Oz*. I didn't know my worth. God had given me a gift, but I didn't take the time to discover the treasure I had inside of me. Instead, I walked in darkness and put myself in harmful situations.

God shifted my focus to the condition of my heart. He allowed me to see myself in the mirror to face my ugliness. But at the same time, while seeing the ugly, I also saw the beauty of who He made me. I began to realize I was gifted. I began to see my worth and value in Christ, realizing I was created for a purpose. I learned the things I was looking for in others—love, acceptance, and validation—I was responsible for providing for myself. No one else's love could rescue me from the loneliness and misery I was feeling; I had to save myself by loving and valuing the person God created me to be. That was my job. Sex couldn't fill the emptiness in my soul. After having sex, I'd still feel unfulfilled; actually, I would feel used and disrespected. But when I began to discover how much God loves me and my true identity in Christ, I began to gain greater confidence and a sense of self-respect. That's when I realized I didn't need so much attention from others and that my value as a person wasn't wrapped up in the clothes I had on and the accessories I carried.

DELIVERANCE

I needed more than anger management classes; I needed deliverance. I don't have anything against therapy and mental health services, but as I mentioned earlier, there's a component in life that most mental health professionals know noth-

CHAPTER 7: WALKING IN THE LIGHT

ing about: the spiritual world. As a result, they don't understand the spiritual power and influence behind many people's actions. And this is where deliverance comes in.

Anger management classes only help you identify the triggers in your life and provide coping skills, but they don't fully get to the root of the problem. Only God could uproot the true source of my anger issues. But that part was a little tricky.

Usually, whenever people talk about deliverance from the power of darkness, they focus on using religion to accomplish this feat. They think that a bunch of religious acts will fix the issue. But unfortunately, many people get caught up in routines and rituals that simply do not work. Or, in some cases, they leave out specific necessary steps highlighted in the Bible. So let me explain what deliverance is.

True biblical deliverance is rooted in obtaining knowledge and revelation. But unfortunately, many people want someone to lay hands on them so they can fall out under the power of God. They believe that if this happens, they'll get up from the floor, and all of their problems will be gone; their habits will instantly disappear, and the negative thoughts and beliefs that circulate in their hearts and minds will evaporate into thin air. But, sadly, once many of these individuals get up from the floor after being prayed over, they return to their seats with the same thoughts still in their hearts and the same doubts in their minds; they have the same habits, tendencies, and self-sabotaging inner beliefs.

As I can attest, the anointing of God is real. I've found myself "slain in the Spirit" many times. But I didn't understand the purpose of the anointing at the time. The Bible explains to us that the anointing of God destroys the chains that keep us bound; however, it doesn't transform our way of thinking. Let me give you an analogy. There was a story of an elephant that was born in captivity. It was being primed to be a circus elephant. The elephant's owner tied a rope around its ankles when it was young, ensuring that it wouldn't stray away from a particular area. Every day, the elephant's training conditioned it mentally to stay in a specific place because of that rope. That rope represents the chains (or "yoke" described in Isaiah 10:27) that keep us bound. Isaiah said the anointing destroys the yoke, the chains. That means the anointing eliminates the power that keeps us bound. However, the actual problem lies in that elephant's thinking. After years of being bound to that spot, that elephant got used to being in that same spot. Once the rope was removed from the elephant's ankles, it remained in that one spot. The physical component that kept it in bondage was removed, but the mental bondage remained. The elephant was physically free to move around, but it didn't realize this. I can use another example: slavery. After slavery was abolished in America, many Blacks decided to remain behind on the plantations; some had no idea the Emancipation Proclamation had just been signed by President Abraham Lincoln, declaring slavery illegal. The slaves who didn't know they were free remained on the plantations, being subjected to inhumane treatment and the worse abuses. Some Blacks continued to live as slaves on plantations throughout the South until the 1960s. Why? It's because they were ignorant (lack of knowledge or awareness) of their rights

CHAPTER 7: WALKING IN THE LIGHT

and the laws of the land. So just because the anointing destroyed the yoke in someone's life doesn't mean they walk in freedom. To walk in freedom, you must become knowledgeable of who you are and your rights in the Kingdom of God. You have to come out of the darkness of ignorance and gain knowledge of God's Word.

It takes the anointing of God and the revelation of God's Word for us to experience true deliverance. First, you need the power of God to break the spiritual chains the enemy has placed on you to keep you in bondage, but then you need the understanding of God's Word to walk out of that place of bondage. The power of God unlocks the prison cell, but knowledge enables us to step out of that cell and into our destinies.

In the beginning, I did everything I believed I needed to do to get free. I fasted. I prayed. I attended deliverance services where people prayed and laid hands on me. But I still had not experienced deliverance. I didn't know that the true bondage was in my thinking and that God had commissioned me to control my thoughts. I didn't realize that I needed to be set free in my mind through the knowledge of God's Word. The Bible says Satan blinds the minds of those who reject the Gospel (2 Corinthians 4:4). Scripture tells us,

> "Instead, let the Spirit renew your thoughts and attitudes" (Ephesians 4:24, NLT).

Also, the Bible says in Romans 12:2,

"Don't copy the behavior and customs of this world, but let God transform you into a new person by changing the way you think. Then you will learn to know God's will for you, which is good and pleasing and perfect" (NLT).

There are so many verses in the Bible where God tells us we have to transform our thought lives if we want to see victory. He informs us the battlefield is in our minds; that's where we must defeat Satan. But the biggest question most people have is, "How do I transform my thinking?" Well, let me explain how to do so.

In 2 Corinthians 10:4, the Apostle Paul wrote,

"We use God's mighty weapons, not worldly weapons, to knock down the strongholds of human reasoning and to destroy false arguments." (NLT)

This reveals to us that it's our responsibility to cast down negative thoughts. God wouldn't instruct us to do this if He didn't give us the authority to execute. As Believers, we've been given power by God to speak to every mountain in our paths (Mark 11:23), including the mountain of wicked thoughts and negative emotions. The Bible states we have power in our tongues, and that power is unleashed through our words (Proverbs 18:21). Therefore, when we speak negativity in our lives, we experience negativity, but when we speak positivity in our lives, we experience positivity. We can either speak life or death over ourselves. We can determine the rest of our day

CHAPTER 7: WALKING IN THE LIGHT

by the words that we speak. The tongue is that powerful; it's our superpower as human beings. Unfortunately, most people use this superpower to curse themselves. They declare themselves to be failures, worthless, no good, defeated and more; they label themselves things God never called them: *I'm sick; I'm schizo; I'm a basket-case; I'm Bipolar; I'm another statistic; I'm poor, and I'll always be poor; I'm stupid; I'm dumb; I'm a slow learner, I'm a little OCD*. One may forget or not know God tells us to acknowledge ourselves according to His Word. And in the Word of God, God says this about us:

> You're healed. You're more than a conqueror through Christ Jesus. You're a brand new creation in Christ. Your body is the temple of the Holy Spirit, not the temple of sickness and disease. You are blessed and highly favored by God. You are the head and not the tail, above and not beneath. God created you to be the lender and not the borrower. You have power over every demonic spirit. You are anointed to win and succeed. You are mighty through Christ. You are victorious in all situations. You are loved by God. You have the mind of Christ. You have the fruit of the Spirit, which contains love, joy, peace, patience, kindness, generosity, faithfulness, gentleness, and self-control. You are fearfully and wonderfully made by God. You are the workmanship of God. You were created in the very image and likeness of God. You are a member of a peculiar people and God's royal priesthood.

Imagine if you spoke these things over yourself daily. In fact, that's what God instructs us to do throughout our daily lives. He tells us to declare His promises over ourselves daily. He instructs us to meditate on His Word so that we can download into our spirits a revelation of who we are and what we have a right to on this earth. God told Joshua,

> "Study this Book of Instruction continually. Meditate on it day and night so you will be sure to obey everything written in it. Only then will you prosper and succeed in all you do" (Joshua 1:8, NLT).

In Hebrew, the word "meditate" is *hāḡâ*, and it means *to speak, imagine, and study*. So daily, we're to study God's Word, speak His promises, and picture ourselves in our minds living out those promises and being who God says we are. Yes, the imagination is powerful. If you envision yourself defeated, you'll be defeated. If you play scenes of you fighting in the club, you'll resort to fighting in the club as soon as someone mistakenly spills their drink on you or bump into you. Your mind controls your body, and the images you play in your head daily determine your body's response to different situations. You must visualize where you're going in life and who you want to become. That's also why the Apostle Paul instructed us to cast down both thoughts and "imaginations" (images; pictures in our minds) that conflict with God's promises. See yourself as blessed, and you'll be blessed. See yourself practicing self-control, and you'll practice self-control in every situation.

CHAPTER 7: WALKING IN THE LIGHT

I constantly claimed I had a bad temper and couldn't control myself, and I always pictured myself fighting and getting into trouble, and lo and behold, everything I said I would be and do, I became, and I did. Finally, I spoke prison up, and I ended up in prison. I spoke of defeat and saw myself defeated, and thus, I experienced failure. I saw myself as a hellion, and therefore, I acted like a hellion. But when I discovered what God said about me, I started gaining a different picture of myself in my mind. And when I started seeing myself differently, I started behaving differently. When I started acting differently, I started getting different results in my life.

Lastly, I want to mention that deliverance is a process and that it doesn't just happen once in our lives. We have to stay at the feet of Christ to remain healed. And during the process of God delivering us—yes, it's a process that doesn't always happen overnight—He's healing us on a deeper level.

A DEEPER HEALING

While writing this book, I can remember God showing me a vision of a dresser—I then heard the words, "Gap between my past." I didn't understand what that meant at first, but I later discovered what God was showing and telling me. He was showing me some hidden things from my past I'd forgotten about, things that were still affecting my heart. God had me revisit when my dad slapped me down for lying to him and my mom about spending the night at a friend's house when I was really at my boyfriend's house. The embarrassment and guilt from that incident stuck with me unknowingly. Next, God began to bring to consciousness many other moments from my past that had remained hidden and locked away in my heart. He was addressing them. But how He dealt with them is crucial. First, God was showing me the power behind those who hurt me. He let me know it wasn't them; it was the enemy operating in and through them.

Furthermore, God was letting me know I didn't cause these things to happen; the enemy set up the traumatic events of my childhood to trap me into a pattern of thinking that would sabotage my future and hinder me from walking in my purpose. Satan knew I was a threat before I realized it, and he moved early on to try to take me out. He knew that if I ever came into knowing who I was and what God had for me, it would be game over for him. So he tried to kill me, he wanted me to kill myself, but God spared me and brought me out of darkness and into His marvelous light to discover who I am and what is rightfully mine and the authority over the enemy God has given. And now, the devil fears me.

The enemy tries to replay old traumatic events in my mind from time to time, and he still speaks lies and negativity into my ears every so often. Still, I know now what he's up to; the devil is upset because he's already defeated and on his way to the lake of fire (Revelation 20:14). He is a defeated foe, and he wants us to experience the same defeat that he's experiencing. He wants to keep us distracted in life rather than focused on God's will for us. He wants us to feel overwhelmed by life's obstacles and look to ourselves for strength rather than turning to God for His strength. He wants us to feel as if we're lacking, incomplete and inadequate. But the Bible says, "For in Him dwells all the fullness of the Godhead bodily; And you are complete in Him, who is the head of all principality and power" (Colossians 2:9-10). So know that you are complete in Christ already. Everything you need to live the life God has called you to is already inside you. Everything you need to be great is within you.

Meditation Verses

"Therefore if any man be in Christ, he is a new creature: old things are passed away; behold, all things are become new." 2 Corinthians 5:17)

"But you are a chosen people, a royal priesthood, a holy nation, God's special possession, that you may declare the praises of him who called you out of darkness into his wonderful light." (1 Peter 2:9, NIV) "

"And you that were sometime alienated and enemies in your mind by wicked works yet now hath he reconciled." (Colossians 1:21)

"[Live] as obedient children [of God]; do not be conformed to the evil desires which governed you in your ignorance [before you knew the requirements and transforming power of the good news regarding salvation]." (1 Peter 1:14)

"God rescued us from the dead-end alleys and dark dungeons. He's set us up in the kingdom of the Son who got us out of the pit we were in, got rid of the sins we were doomed to keep repeating." (Col 1:13-14, The Message Translation)

"Satan, who is the god of this world, has blinded the minds of those who don't believe. They are unable to see the glorious light of the Good News. They don't understand this message about the glory of Christ, who is the exact likeness of God." 2 Corinthians 4:4, NLT)

"For you have rescued me from death; you have kept my feet from slipping. So now I can walk in your presence, O God, in your life-giving light." (Psalm 56:13, NLT)

"And he did rescue us from mortal danger, and he will rescue us again. We have placed our confidence in him, and he will continue to rescue us." (2 Corinthians 1:10, NLT)

"And we know that God causes everything to work together[fn] for the good of those who love God and are called according to his purpose for them." (Romans 8:28, NLT)

Prayer

Dear Heavenly Father, I thank you for delivering me from the darkness and bringing me into your glorious light. I am a brand new creation in Christ, old things have passed away and all things have been made new. Continue to transform my thinking and teach me your ways. Let me live as Christ lived, walk as He walked, and do as Christ did. Today, I totally surrender to you and ask you to order my steps and lead me. I thank you that all things are currently working together for my good. It's in Jesus' name I pray. Amen.

BLACKOUT

Final Words

To be called out of darkness is to understand the new life Christ has given us and to walk in that new life. Your old way of living should no longer define you. There's a grace available that allows you to overcome every obstacle. You've been trying to work for what is already done and provided to you by Christ Jesus, but now it's time to stop working and start resting in the finished work of Christ.

There's so much God wants to download into your spirit, as He did mine. One day, he spoke to me about going to New York and said I'd be traveling there soon. He also spoke to me about becoming a bestselling author. He revealed to me that I'd be traveling and speaking, that I'd be touching lives all over the world, and that I'd make His name (the name of Jesus) famous. There's so much God has shown me and spoken into my heart.

Living with a God-sized dream on the inside of you, waking up daily knowing that you are about to shoot to the moon and stars and do great things, living each day in anticipation of the great things God is about to do in your life, that's what it looks like living in the light! It looks like a life of joy, anticipation of good things, hope, confidence, awareness of who you are in Christ Jesus, healing, peace, and divine power. Rather than having a life dominated by dark clouds of fear, the bright sunlight of the Good News and divine promises will permeate your life.

I want to end with these sayings. The first is a passage of Scripture from Job 11:13-20, the Message Translation. The second is a series of affirmations I would like you to read and speak over yourself to align with God's will and purpose.

"Still, if you set your heart on God
    and reach out to him,
If you scrub your hands of sin
    and refuse to entertain evil in your home,
You'll be able to face the world unashamed
    and keep a firm grip on life, guiltless and fearless.
You'll forget your troubles;
    they'll be like old, faded photographs.
Your world will be washed in sunshine,
    every shadow dispersed by dawn.
Full of hope, you'll relax, confident again;
    you'll look around, sit back, and take it easy.
Expansive, without a care in the world,
    you'll be hunted out by many for your blessing.
But the wicked will see none of this.

They're headed down a dead-end road
with nothing to look forward to—nothing."

DECREES FOR TODAY:

- When I stopped "hating on me," rejection lost its power and authority in my life.
- I found true LOVE, that's when I stopped "hating on me".
- What was cloudy became clear when I stopped "hating on me".
- When I was "hating on me," I didn't believe what God said about me.
- I was able to "forgive me" when I stopped believing the lies of the devil.
- Bye to self-hate!
- Bye to self-rejection!
- Bye to self-deception!
- Bye to insecurity!
- Bye to inferiority!
- Bye to envy!
- Bye to jealousy!
- Bye to comparison!
- Bye to competition!
- Bye to lust for recognition!
- I give up my security!
- I give up my safety in obscurity!

- I give up my vulnerability!
- I choose not to walk in deception, deceiving myself and others and being deceived by others!
- I trust God to protect me!
- I choose to tear down every stronghold through the power of God that has me bound!
- I choose not to be conformed to this world but be transformed by the renewing of my mind!
- I choose to walk in the image of God, and not by the images of this fallen world!
- I choose to love me for me with my flaws and all!
- Today's breakthrough, I celebrate only because He first LOVED me! Thank You, Father God!
- The Blood of Jesus works!
- Without the shedding of blood, there is no forgiveness of sins.
- I'm walking in the newness of life!

www.ingramcontent.com/pod-product-compliance
Lightning Source LLC
LaVergne TN
LVHW041710060526
838201LV00043B/660